Few people are making jokes about the church these days. Most Christians are dead serious about their churches. Where they are growing, people are excited and anxious to do their part to keep things moving for the glory of God. Where they are declining, people want to know the reasons why and what they can do about it.

Finding the answers to the question of why churches are growing or not growing is what the Church Growth Movement is all about. There are many different ways of approaching the task of discovering what God is doing in today's world. And one of them is to look around the country at the churches that seem to be doing something unusual and, consequently, are maintaining a steady pattern of growth.

Just what is it that makes churches like these grow? Of course, it is, in the final analysis, God at work through His Holy Spirit. But if we prayerfully study these churches and others like them, we can discover more and more about the way God works and the way He builds His Kingdom.

And that is what this book is all about.

—C.P.W.

Your Church can Grow

C. PETER WAGNER

Regal Books
A Division of GL Publications
Ventura, California, U S A

Published by Regal Books
A Division of GL Publications
Ventura, California 93006
Printed in U.S.A.

Library of Congress Cataloging in Publication Data

Wagner, C. Peter.
   Your church can grow.

   Includes index.
   1. Church growth.   I. Wimber, John.   II. Title.
BV652.25.W332   1984   254'.5   84-8314
ISBN 0-8037-0978-9

4 5 6 7 8 9 10 / 91 90 89 88 87

Rights for publishing this book in other languages are contracted by Gospel
Literature International (GLINT) foundation. GLINT also provides technical
help for the adaptation, translation, and publishing of Bible study resources
and books in scores of languages worldwide. For further information, contact
GLINT, Post Office Box 488, Rosemead, California, 91770, U.S.A., or the
publisher.

Other Books by C. Peter Wagner

What Are We Missing? (Creation House)

Your Spiritual Gifts Can Help Your Church Grow (Regal Books)

Our Kind of People: The Ethical Dimensions of Church Growth in America (John Knox Press)

Your Church Can Be Healthy (Abingdon)

Church Growth and the Whole Gospel: A Biblical Mandate (Harper & Row)

Effective Body Building: Biblical Steps to Spiritual Growth (Here's Life Publishers)

Helping Your Church Grow (audio cassettes) (David C. Cook Publishing Co.)

On the Crest of the Wave: Becoming a World Christian (Regal Books)

Leading Your Church to Growth: The Secret of Pastor/People Partnership in Dynamic Church Growth (Regal Books)

Bible Study Guide

Readers of this book will be glad to know that an accompanying 8½-by-11 inch, 70-page Bible study guide/workbook is available for use in seminars and classroom situations. If interested, write: Charles E. Fuller Institute of Evangelism and Church Growth, P.O. Box 91990, Pasadena, California 91109-1990, and request, "Your Church Can Grow Bible Study Guide."

DEDICATED
TO
PAUL CEDAR,
THE PASTORAL STAFF,
AND MY CHRISTIAN BROTHERS AND SISTERS
IN LAKE AVENUE CONGREGATIONAL CHURCH
PASADENA, CALIFORNIA

CONTENTS

Introduction

WHERE DID CHURCH GROWTH COME FROM?

"Evangelicals from all points on the ecclesiological con-
tinuum agree: the Church Growth Movement is 'hot,' the
debate it has stirred is getting hotter, and evangelicals
around the world—not just those in the U.S.—are going
to have to deal with it."

With these words, Robert Coote of *Eternity* magazine
introduces a special report on what he considers to be
"one of the most stimulating, yet controversial developments in today's church."

This is a book about that "hot" movement. It is one of
the first systematic attempts to apply the scientific principles of church growth as developed by Donald McGavran
specifically to the American scene. In one sense it is overdue. In fact the impact of the whole Church Growth Movement on America is overdue.

When this book was first published in 1976 the Church
Growth Movement was barely twenty years old, but it had
only become known among American church leaders over
a period of a year or two. Since most of us Americans are
conditioned—rather ethnocentrically—to "hot" ideas

being generated in the U.S. and then exported abroad, this reversal comes as a surprise.

It would be a mistake to imagine that only evangelicals are taking an interest in church growth philosophy as a helpful and creative way of analyzing American religion. Many of the mainline churches as well are asking for accurate insights as to why some churches grow and why some decline.

For one thing, the alarming decline in membership in most U.S. mainline denominations which began in the mid-sixties has made their leaders sit up and take notice. Over the ten-year period 1971-1981, for example, the Reformed Church in America declined 6 percent, the United Methodist Church declined 10 percent, the United Church of Christ declined 11 percent, the Episcopal Church declined 15 percent, the Disciples of Christ declined 17 percent, and the United Presbyterian Church declined 21 percent. Some of these denominations which were rather cavalier about membership loss in the early seventies are talking survival in the eighties. A few are rather cautiously approaching the Church Growth Movement to see if they can discover some clues for positive action.

One of the factors that has encouraged them is a period of testing that church growth principles have passed through. Back in 1976 the "seven vital signs of a healthy church," which this book explains, were brand new. A good bit of the testing has been informal and anecdotal. But at least five academically-oriented computerized tests have been made by researchers, and the seven vital signs have held up well. The one such test which has been published was conducted among British Baptist churches by Paul Beasley-Murray and Alan Wilkinson. Their book is *Turning the Tide* (British Bible Society, 1981). In it they show that five of the seven signs are clearly positive. The other two (a large enough church and the homogeneous unit principle) lacked sufficient data to test out one way or the other.

WHERE CHURCH GROWTH COMES FROM

Church growth as a movement entered North America in the fall of 1972. It took root in the mind and ministry of Donald McGavran while he was serving as a third-generation missionary to India over a period of thirty years. His first attempts at putting his ideas into writing date back to 1936.

But the widespread diffusion of the movement began with the publication of *The Bridges of God* (Friendship Press, 1955) and *How Churches Grow* (Friendship Press, 1959). These brought church growth, as it applied to *world* evangelization, to national and international attention. The books were extensively reviewed in missionary journals on both sides of the Atlantic and around the world.

How Churches Grow did attempt to address church growth in America. One of its chapters was reprinted as a booklet under the title *Do Churches Grow?* It sold thousands of copies among American church leaders, but failed to light any fires. The time was not yet ripe.

"CHURCH GROWTH" DEFINED

The term *church growth* is a McGavranism. At first, McGavran attempted to phrase the insights he had developed using more traditional language such as "evangelism" or "missions," but he soon found that these terms were little more than useless. They had been defined and redefined so much that they had lost their cutting edge. When "evangelism" and "missions" came to mean everything good that Christians did individually and collectively, they then meant practically nothing.

So in order to describe, in a precise way, what he was

trying to articulate, Donald McGavran took two common words and welded them together. Now "church growth," as a technical phrase, is as independent from "church" and "growth" as "Grape Nuts" is from "grapes" and "nuts." Actually "church growth" means *all that is involved in bringing men and women who do not have a personal relationship to Jesus Christ into fellowship with Him and into responsible church membership.*

THE INSTITUTE OF CHURCH GROWTH

After the publication of *The Bridges of God* and *How Churches Grow,* McGavran found himself in high demand as a speaker and seminar leader. He soon realized, however, that such an itinerant ministry would exert only a minimal influence on the world of missions. So he decided to establish a new institution designed to bring together career missionaries on furlough. They would study and master church growth principles on a graduate level, field test them, and transfer the concepts to others. They would also learn the research methodology needed to discover new principles.

The Institute of Church Growth grew out of that vision, and Northwest Christian College in Eugene, Oregon, offered both sponsorship and hospitality. McGavran's own background in the Christian Church made the association a natural, and classes began there in 1961.

It wasn't long, however, until the institute outgrew its first home. In 1965 it moved to Fuller Theological Seminary in Pasadena, California, where it became the School of World Mission and Institute of Church Growth.

McGavran's school is now just short of twenty years old. Already in his sixty-eighth year when he founded the school, he led it through its formative stages in the sixties. Arthur F. Glasser was dean through the decade of the seventies, and Paul E. Pierson is currently dean. The full-time faculty includes ten persons all with overseas missionary experience. Two of us, Eddie Gibbs and I, specialize in the field of church growth. The School of World Mission continues to furnish an institutional base for the worldwide Church Growth Movement, while the Doctor of Ministry program in the Fuller School of Theology provides an outstanding graduate program for American church growth.

THE OBJECTIVE OF CHURCH GROWTH

Some people do not realize that McGavran developed the theory of church growth and founded his institution with a precisely defined objective: to make more effective the propagation of the gospel and the multiplication of churches *on new ground*. He believed that the expenditure of $1 billion a year out of North America for overseas missions could be made to yield much more Christianization. To this end he planned to spread the church growth school of thought among mission executives, career missionaries, and national church leaders working in Asia, Africa, and Latin America.

McGavran recognized, of course, that church growth principles apply universally; but he decided to concentrate on the tremendous population overseas. He illustrated his principles almost entirely from missions and new denominations overseas. Consequently the Christian workers dedicated to ministry in Canada and the United States who attended his classes or seminars or read his books, did not usually think of church growth as applying to America.

Launching Church Growth in America

Interestingly, when McGavran was teaching missions in the seminaries of the Christian Church in the late 1950s, his students preparing for American ministry frequently said to him, "The principles you teach apply here."

He would reply, "Yes, they do, but how they apply will have to be worked out by you."

So until 1972, church growth continued to appear chiefly applicable to other lands. A top-level American evangelical leader once said to me, "Somehow I never knew what church growth was. I always thought it was just something out there on the mission field."

He sounded as if he felt he had been slightly cheated. Maybe he had been!

It should be noticed, however, that some lack of interest in church growth was largely conditioned by defensive thinking. This rationale maintained on many grounds that the true Christian is not interested in mere numbers.

Since many American churches were not growing, church leaders and seminary professors had constructed an extensive defense, partly theological, *against* church growth. This position glorified smallness and "quality" and maintained that growth in numbers is somewhat disreputable. One of McGavran's great contributions has been his thirty-year assault on this non-biblical position.

His magnum opus, *Understanding Church Growth* (Eerdmans), was published in 1970 and in a revised edition in 1980. It played a part in preparing America for church growth. It treats church growth on a global basis, vigorously exposes the fallacy of defensive thinking, and states the universal principles which characterize it. McGavran first illustrated growth principles almost entirely from the expansion of churches overseas, but he has included many American applications in the 1980 revision. It is and will long be the principal and indispensable textbook for the Church Growth Movement.

Applying Church Growth in America

The conscious attempt to apply church growth philoso phy to America was stimulated in the fall of 1972 by Pastor

Chuck Miller, then a staff member of Pasadena's Lake Avenue Congregational Church, where I have my membership. At Miller's urging, I organized and invited Donald McGavran to team-teach with me a pilot course in church growth designed specifically for American church leaders.

We did it only as an experiment, but the results were remarkable:

One of the students, Win Arn, left his position with the Evangelical Covenant Church and founded the influential Institute for American Church Growth.

Chuck Miller himself resigned his position at Lake Avenue Church and enrolled in the School of World Mission to move deeper into what for him was a fascinating field of study.

Phil Goble, another student, used the insights he received in the class to develop a creative model for Jewish evangelism which he more appropriately calls "synagogue growth." Since then he has helped establish five Messianic synagogues in California, Florida, and New York.

Promoting Church Growth in America

Apparently, the time was ripe. A few years previously, with all the social turmoil in the U.S.A., American church leaders had not been so receptive to church growth teaching. One of the first advocates of the idea was Wade Coggins of the Evangelical Foreign Missions Association, who wrote in the March, 1967 issue of *United Evangelical Action:* "Up to now, church growth research and training have been aimed toward the missionary front. What about pastors in the U.S.? Should they not be equally interested and equally in need of this philosophy and emphasis? . . . A way must be found to gather the facts on significant growth in this country and disseminate this information to stimulate the church into dynamic growth."

But apparently, few in the turbulent sixties were able to hear what Wade Coggins was saying over the din of the civil rights controversies, the hippie movement, and the Viet Nam war.

Two prominent American publishers gave a significant boost to church growth in America during that pivotal year of 1972. The first was William Petersen of *Eternity* Magazine, who sent me a collection of books and magazine clippings he had accumulated and asked me for an article on the subject. I wanted to write the article but I couldn't do it because I simply did not know that much about the American church and how it grows.

It took me almost two years to gain enough understanding of the church in my own native land to fulfill the assignment, but the product of the research was very well received. It was published not only in *Eternity,* but also in *United Evangelical Action* and other places. The National Association of Evangelicals did an offprint under the title "American Church Growth" and circulated thousands of that printing.

This book evolved as a further development of the same research project. American church growth has now become a permanent part of my scholarly interests, and I have published several additional books on the subject.

Harold Lindsell of *Christianity Today* was the second publisher to nudge church growth theoreticians towards America. "If this is the Fuller School of *World* Mission," he once said to a meeting of the faculty, "I want to know if you consider America to be a part of the *world?*"

When the answer was affirmative, he challenged the School of World Mission faculty to apply their insights to the developing nationwide Key 73 evangelistic program, and offered the entire January 19, 1973, issue of *Christianity Today* as a platform. All six faculty members accepted the challenge and contributed essays. But response was minimal, and the effort turned out to be too little too late to rescue Key 73 from evangelistic impotence. It did serve, however, to inform the Christian public that the Church Growth Movement had come back home.

PROFESSIONAL CONSULTATION FOR GROWTH

One of the most exciting developments in the emerging field of American church growth is the creation of a new kind of Christian vocation: the professional church growth consultant. Church consultants have been around for some time, but this is a new breed. It is a kind of consultant trained to see how all the varied parts of church life and ministry can come together to stimulate membership growth.

The pioneer in the field was Pastor John Wimber who resigned his position in Yorba Linda Friends Church in 1975 to become the founding director of what is now called the Charles E. Fuller Institute of Evangelism and Church Growth, located in Pasadena, California. A successful businessperson before his conversion and call to the ministry, Wimber brought a very important credential to church growth: he had been a successful American pastor. His Yorba Linda Friends Church had leveled out at two hundred members when he joined the staff. In five years it had grown to nine hundred and he had helped plant five new Friends churches in the area during the same period of time.

After building the Fuller Institute into a nationally recognized service agency in two years, Wimber felt the call of God to plant a new church, the Vineyard Christian Fellowship of Anaheim. In seven years it grew from an initial seventeen to over five thousand. As his successor he trained Carl F. George, a Baptist pastor from Florida. Carl George has now become the dean of church growth con-

sultants in America and runs the nation's only formal training program for them. Between sixty and seventy of his
students are now helping churches across the country. His
program, called Diagnosis with Impact, is a ministry of the
Charles E. Fuller Institute (Box 91990, Pasadena, CA
91109-1990).

THE FUTURE OF CHURCH GROWTH

The United States has about 330 thousand churches.
There are another 20 thousand in Canada. Of them, how
many are hurting? How many could reverse discouraging
patterns of stagnation and decline and begin to grow if
they just had the help to do it?

Could there be 50 thousand? 100 thousand? If so, we
must trust God to multiply the Win Arns, the John Wim-
bers, and the Carl Georges, for no one person has the full
answer to all the problems of American churches.

There is no such thing as a panacea for all ills, whether
human or church. And church growth itself is a young science, so its contribution as yet is necessarily limited. Progress will require hard work and full dedication, for understanding and analyzing the dynamics of church growth is a
complex matter.

I see a new day dawning for the American church. Tremendous human and spiritual powers, now locked into
restrictive patterns and outmoded methodologies, will
soon be released for the accelerated spread of the Kingdom of God on our continent. If so, all those who love the
Lord and are willing to serve Him are in for exciting times!

C. Peter Wagner
Fuller Theological Seminary
Pasadena
January, 1984

Chapter 1

TO GROW OR NOT TO GROW?

Coral Ridge Presbyterian Church: You are en route to Fort Lauderdale, Florida. But you don't drive for long on North Federal Highway before you see in the distance the 303-foot tower of the Coral Ridge Presbyterian Church. And when you spot it, you have identified the tallest building between the rocket launching pads of Cape Canaveral and the city of Miami.

The $6 million Coral Ridge structure was originally designed to seat twenty-five hundred so that the whole congregation could worship together at 11:00 on Sunday mornings. However, the church had already grown so much between the drawing of the plans and the dedication of the building that two services were needed from the beginning.

Many factors are contributing to the growth of Coral Ridge Presbyterian. Not the least of them is a dedicated, gifted, well-trained corps of four hundred men and women who move out from the church week after week seeking unsaved people and introducing them to Jesus Christ.

Pastor James Kennedy long ago found that growth in

his church had been stifled because the people had the attitude that the pastor should do all the evangelism. He now says, "Letting clerical George do it is the greatest heresy that has plagued the church!"

A film that dramatizes what is going on in Fort Lauderdale is entitled, *Like a Mighty Army.* Spend a week in Fort Lauderdale, and you will see that the army is for real.

Redwood Chapel: Let's now visit Redwood Chapel in Castro Valley, California near San Francisco. In Fort Lauderdale you found a stately worship service with the ministers in full academic regalia and the ushers all dressed in sky blue tuxedos with black velvet trim. In Castro Valley the only specially dressed people are those involved in the musical groups.

Probably few churches in the country have developed the variety of professional-quality small singing groups that you see and hear in Redwood Chapel. The music is so good that church members invite their neighbors to church with no reservations. They know their friends will like it.

Their sanctuary which seats 650 is packed out at each of the three Sunday morning services. When the crowds get too big, large groups of them hive off and start new churches in the area. The new churches develop new musical groups and the new neighbors like it. Many of them are introduced to Jesus Christ, and the daughter churches are growing as well as the mother.

Denver First Nazarene: A mile high in Denver, Colorado, the Denver First Church of the Nazarene has grown from 240 members to 1900 over the past sixteen years. When Pastor Don Wellman went to Denver sixteen years ago, he had set a goal of building a great church for God. He knew that churches can become involved in lots of good activities, but he and his people were single-minded. He says, "We're only interested in one thing—sharing the claims of the gospel with the world."

The world seems to be attracted to the claims of the gospel that First Nazarene presents. In 1974 they moved out of their old building into a 3,800-seat sanctuary. Often three thousand gather for worship on a Sunday morning.

Pastor Wellman has an eight-point program he is implementing: prayer, youth, music, outreach, education, personal evangelism, senior citizens, and Sunday service programs.

First Baptist, Hammond: On Sunday mornings, Hammond, Indiana and surrounding communities are virtually crawling with blue buses bearing the motto: "World's Largest Sunday School" across their sides. If you don't know where the church is, you can soon get the directions from one of the two hundred bus captains you are bound to meet. Special duty policemen from the Hammond Police Department need to be assigned to the neighborhood of First Baptist Church on Sunday mornings to direct the traffic. Over five thousand people crowd in to hear Pastor Jack Hyles.

The area where the church is located in downtown Hammond is no suburban country club setting. It is typical inner city: run-down, slightly depressed. Many stores and businesses have vacated their buildings, but if it's near the church no sooner does a store get vacated than First Baptist moves in and converts it to Sunday School classrooms.

The First Baptist folks need all the space they can get. One week in 1976 they set a national record with 101 thousand people out to Sunday School. They averaged 18,504 weekly during 1982. Over eight hundred trained Sunday School teachers minister every Sunday.

Chapel Hill Harvester: You drive out Flat Shoals Road through the Atlanta suburb of Decatur, Georgia, and you wonder what you are seeing. A huge blue and white tent grabs your attention, and you soon realize it is a church. This is not a fly-by-night evangelist or faith healer but a local church called Chapel Hill Harvester Church. If you are there on Sunday morning you will see five thousand people crowding into the tent celebrating the glory of God in a service lasting over two hours. The color of the audience is as impressive as the color of the tent—about half are white and half black.

Leading the service is the founder of the church, Bishop Earl P. Paulk. He and some family members started the church as an inner city mission in Atlanta in 1960. A total of thirty-nine attended the first service, twelve of whom were family members. They moved from Atlanta to Decatur in 1971 and built a sanctuary on six acres of land. Not only have they outgrown the sanctuary and moved into the tent, but they have purchased a total of eighty-nine acres and are developing what they are calling the "City of Refuge," showcased by a four-thousand-seat sanctuary.

Chapel Hill's ministry concentrates on the needs of the individual members and of the surrounding community. Their extensive social service program attracts hundreds and hundreds of people to the place where they can hear the gospel of Jesus Christ. Their House of New Life, for example, is designed to provide a viable alternative to unwed mothers who find themselves in a society which sees abortion as the only solution to their problem. In His Care is a licensed child placement agency which serves the entire Christian community. Special programs address the needs of prisoners, divorced people, the chemically addicted, homosexuals, compulsive overeaters, senior citizens, the physically and mentally handicapped, and other similar groups.

Southern California: Growing churches like these, which can be found in every region of the United States, are thrilling to visit. It builds Christian faith to see God's hand at work through His people in so many different places, in so many different denominations, and in so many different ways. One of the heaviest concentrations of growing churches is to be found in Southern California, where I live and work. I would love to take you on a guided tour of some of the most exciting churches I have seen, all located just a relatively short drive from each other.

I would take you to the Crystal Cathedral, formerly known as Garden Grove Community Church. You would be there with eight thousand other people worshiping in a breathtaking sanctuary made of ten thousand pieces of glass. You would hear a sermon highlighting "possibility thinking" from Pastor Robert Schuller. Schuller and his wife, Arvella, started the church from scratch twenty-nine years ago, preaching from the tar-papered roof of the Orange Drive-in Theater.

Then we would go to Melodyland Christian Center, near Disneyland, where Pastor Ralph Wilkerson ministers with great power, and where thousands upon thousands of people have been saved through the years.

We would visit Calvary Chapel of Costa Mesa where we would have to stand in line twenty minutes before any of the three services in order to get one of the three thousand seats in the sanctuary. We would see Pastor Chuck Smith, whom God used as one of the initiators of the Jesus People Movement in the sixties, and who in those days was creative enough to hold services in a tent and baptize converts in the Pacific Ocean.

Then we would go down the coastline to Saddleback Valley Community Church of Laguna Hills, one of the most innovative Southern Baptist Churches in the nation. Pastor Rick Warren, who started the church fresh out of seminary in 1980, has set a growth goal of no less than twenty thousand members by the year 2000 while at the same time pioneering a new church each year. The growth is right on schedule.

On Sunday evening I would take you to Vineyard Christian Fellowship in Anaheim, pastored by my colleague John Wimber. It meets in a former White Front department store. Your eyes would widen as you walked in and saw the vast expanse of three thousand folding chairs, all of them full, mostly with young people. Before the evening was over, probably one hundred persons would be touched directly by God for physical, emotional, and spiritual healing.

We could stop in at First Evangelical Free Church of Fullerton to hear some of the best Bible exposition in the U.S. from Pastor Charles Swindoll. The day the congregation moved into its twenty-five-hundred-seat sanctuary, three years ago, both morning services were full to overflowing. A relatively short drive over the freeways would take us to Grace Community Church of the Valley in Panorama City where another renowned Bible expositor, John MacArthur, is teaching the Word. There we would join eight thousand others in the worship services.

I wouldn't want you to miss Calvary Community of Thousand Oaks. Seven years ago Pastor Larry DeWitt began meeting with a handful of people in the Hungry Tiger restaurant. Now worship is running over two thousand in a leased warehouse. They have purchased thirty acres on a major freeway intersection and are drawing up plans for an enormous sanctuary.

For a change of atmosphere we would visit Bel Air Presbyterian Church, a spectacular piece of architecture built on the edge of a cliff overlooking Los Angeles. There Pastor Donn Moomaw sees a hundred to two hundred so-called "up and outers" commit their lives to Jesus Christ every year.

SOME GROW AND SOME DO NOT

I could go on and on citing other examples of growing

churches. But these I have mentioned already are sufficient to indicate that some churches in the United States are indeed growing. Pastors and people in them are excited about being Christians and working for God. The Lord is adding daily such as should be saved—even as He did in the First Church of Jerusalem described in the book of Acts.

Just what is it that makes some churches grow?

And why are other churches dead on the vine? For it is a fact that many churches are dead. They haven't grown in years. For every new family that comes in, two or three go out. Attending church is a chore—something to get over with as soon as possible before settling down to a more enjoyable activity like watching the pro football game on television.

Statistics show that some denominations are growing while others are declining. From one year to the next, for example, the Christian and Missionary Alliance, the Church of God (Cleveland), the Church of the Nazarene, the Assemblies of God, the Southern Baptists and others seem to grow well, while during the same year the United Methodists, the Disciples of Christ, the Episcopal Church, the Presbyterians, the American Lutherans and others decline.

But even that pattern is not uniform. Many Methodist, Presbyterian, and Lutheran churches are growing, and many Alliance, Nazarene, and Southern Baptist churches are losing membership.

Sometimes these churches are close to one another. In case after case the struggling, discouraged churches find themselves within only two or three blocks of sister churches which are thriving. It is not uncommon in America for church members to drive past a half dozen other churches to get to the church of their choice. And their church hardly differs at all in doctrine from many of the other churches they pass. However, even though God is present in all of these churches, their own church offers something the others don't seem to have.

There are no particular regions of America that can be considered the promised land for growth. I used to think that California was the place where churches grew like dandelions on a golf course while New England was barren soil. I now realize it is much more complex than that. Southern Baptist churches, for example, are growing more rapidly in New England than in California, although some years ago it was the other way around. California may have more than its share of flamboyant, headline-grabbing churches, but when it comes to statistics, California has a higher percentage of unchurched people than New England!

Why? Why? Why?

Is there any sense to all this?

Why do some churches grow while others do not?

The answer to this question is so elusive that many church leaders even hesitate to raise it.

Back in the sixties, as most of us remember all too well, many had even begun to question whether the church *should* grow. There was doubt in some minds as to whether the church could ever be a benefit to society as a whole. For a while it became fashionable in certain circles to proclaim that we now live in a "post-Christian age." The institutional church was considered outmoded.

Some overhang from the sixties still persists like a pesky cough after a hard cold. But by and large, church growth has edged up toward the top of the agenda in churches across the board.

The Christian and Missionary Alliance agreed in 1979 to set a goal of doubling their total membership by 1987, a remarkable public declaration of faith. As this is being written midway in the process, the growth is right on target.

The Evangelical Covenant churches have recently rallied around a "Giving for Growing" project to the tune of contributing several million dollars over and above their regular church commitment. They have created a new denominational office: Director of Church Growth. They definitely want Covenant churches to grow. Some Presbyterian and Episcopalian and other mainline churches are requesting church growth seminars, dissatisfied with their present trends.

Yes, few people are making jokes about the church these days. Most Christians I know are dead serious about their churches. Where they are growing, people are excited and anxious to do their part to keep things moving for the glory of God. Where they are declining, people want to know the reasons why and what they can do about it.

Finding the answers to the question of why churches are growing or not growing is what the Church Growth Movement is all about. No one has the final word, but good answers are surfacing with increasing frequency.

There are many different ways of approaching the task of discovering what God is doing in today's world. And one of them—as we are doing here—is to look around the country at the churches that seem to be doing something unusual and, consequently, are maintaining a steady pattern of growth. And while we look at them, we ask again our original question: *Just what is it that makes churches like these grow?*

Of course, it is, in the final analysis, God at work through His Holy Spirit. But if we study these churches and others like them with "church growth eyes," we can learn more about God and the way He works.

You see, if I need to study harvesting procedures, I want to be where production is "thirty, sixty and a hun-

dredfold," as the Bible says (Matt. 13:8). By the same
token, if I want to learn more about why churches grow, I
can hardly do better than to study growing churches.

How They Do It

Others also believe we can learn from these churches.
In fact, many of the pastors of growing churches have
received so many calls for help that they have organized
how-we-do-it seminars—held one to four times a year on
their church campuses. Every March, for example, Jack
Hyles of First Baptist, Hammond holds a Pastors' School.
In 1974 the school drew 2,311 participants. By 1983 it was
drawing 5,000.

Pastor Robert Schuller of the Crystal Cathedral leads
the Institute for Successful Church Leadership, which I
am personally biased toward because I have taught in it for
many years. Its president, Herman Ridder, schedules
three sessions of the institute every year.

One of the best training courses in the country for
techniques of personal evangelism is the Evangelism
Explosion clinic held at the Coral Ridge Presbyterian
Church. It is multiplied in clinics across the nation.

Pastor Jerry Falwell of Thomas Road Baptist Church,
Lynchburg, Virginia holds an annual "Super Conference"
for pastors and Christian workers. Total attendance usually runs around sixty-five hundred including church leaders, Liberty Baptist College students and about fifteen
hundred pastors from outside.

In Fresno, California, G.L. Johnson, pastor of People's
Church, conducts a fall seminar on Church Management
and Christian leadership.

W.A. Criswell, pastor of First Baptist, Dallas, Texas,
covers every area of ministry in his annual School of the
Prophets.

Pastor Larry DeWitt of Calvary Community, Thousand

Oaks sets aside one day per month to share the methods God has used for growth with any pastors and lay leaders who wish to attend.

Ray Stedman teaches the body life principles of Peninsula Bible Church, Palo Alto, California in a two-week internship program.

Pastor William E. Yaeger of First Baptist, Modesto, California convenes his Institute of Church Imperatives three times a year. He emphasizes leadership and the practical how-to's of the ministry.

The tuition costs for these non-academic training opportunities run from nothing to $200. And though they will never substitute for a seminary education, I believe they should receive more of a place in supplementing ministerial training than they have up to the present time.

CHURCH GROWTH IS COMPLEX

Even when we put together all that is taught in these seminars, we recognize that we still have a great deal to learn about why some churches grow and some don't. Simply put, *church growth is complex.* There is no way it can be reduced to a simple formula or a canned program.

W.A. Criswell, for example, credits the growth of First Baptist, Dallas largely to expository preaching of the Word. But Robert Schuller rarely preaches an expository message. His topical messages communicate "possibility thinking" to unbelievers who know nothing about the Bible and care little whether they do.

James Kennedy will single out house-to-house visitation as the most effective means for growth in Florida, but Stephen Olford tried it in New York City to no avail. He depends more on penetrating the high-rises through television.

Richard Halverson found that developing small koinonia groups is his best approach in Washington D.C. Wendell Belew of the Southern Baptist Home Mission Board, however, once told me of two churches that "died of koinonia"!

Jack Hyles argues that building his Sunday School through busing helps his whole church grow, but Paul Cedar's church sold its last Sunday School bus some years ago and grew faster after it did.

Qualities of Church Growth Leaders

While the patterns of church growth in America and elsewhere may be complex, they are not chaotic: A considerable degree of expertise is accumulating among those who have entered the field of church growth on a professional basis. And those who do so usually have combined a certain set of personal qualities which give a kind of identity to church growth leaders.

Here are five of them. In other words, if you meet a church growth leader, you can recognize him or her by:

1. *Single-minded obedience.* Church growth leaders take the Lordship of Jesus Christ very seriously. They have counted, as Dietrich Bonhoeffer would say, "the cost of discipleship." They are willing to pay the price for doing whatever is necessary to obey and fulfill God's Great Commission (Matt. 28:19-20). They are fully aware that a steward's faithfulness will ultimately be evaluated by the result of the efforts, and they have a deep desire to hear those coveted words on the last day: "Well done, good and faithful servant" (Matt. 25:21).

2. *Clearly defined objectives.* Church growth leaders are motivated by the assurance that they have understood the revealed will of God for world evangelization and that they are attuned to what God expects to accomplish through them. Thus, they are not reluctant to set measurable goals and to allow their success or failure to be evaluated in light of these goals, risky as this procedure might

seem to those unfamiliar with church growth objectives.

They have long since rejected counting "decisions" or those who "pray to receive Jesus" as criteria for evaluating evangelistic success. They are interested only in *disciples,* validated primarily through commitment to Jesus Christ as Lord and to responsible membership in a Christian church.

3. *Reliance on discerning research.* Church growth leaders are well aware of what must have been behind the words of Proverbs 18:13 (*TLB*): "What a shame—yes, how stupid!—to decide before knowing the facts!" All too much Christian work is undertaken stupidly simply because the facts of the situation are not adequately known.

Present research methodology leaves much room for improvement; nevertheless, substantial advances have been made in the field. More and more is becoming known about how to plan intelligently for church growth, and research efforts are being accelerated.

4. *Ruthlessness in evaluating results.* Church growth leaders have often been criticized as being too pragmatic. They are pragmatic, but they would like to consider it as *consecrated* pragmatism.

If methods currently being used for some evangelistic effort, for example, are not accomplishing the stated goals, they must be revised or scrapped. A strategy must be substituted that will produce the results that God desires.

Church growth is an activist's philosophy. Little wonder that those who prefer to be passive and "leave the results to God" argue that shrinking churches are likely to be the most faithful churches and write books like Robert Hudnut's *Church Growth Is Not the Point* (Harper & Row). It goes without saying that such a thesis is unacceptable to church growth people.

5. *An attitude of optimism and faith.* Church growth leaders are not intimidated by the charge that they are "triumphalists." They are convinced that Christ is building His church as He said He would (see Matt. 16:18), and they are confident that the gates of hell will not prevail against it. They are excited about participating in the building of the church worldwide and they rejoice when churches grow and multiply.

They pray for conversions in large numbers. They expect God to bring about people movements to Christ. Their New Testament paradigm for evangelism is not the rich young ruler, but the day of Pentecost where three thousand came to Christ and "continued steadfastly in the apostles' doctrine and fellowship, in the breaking of bread, and in prayers" (Acts 2:42). They believe that this is pleasing to God because it is a product of faith.

What Are the Vital Signs?

When the mentality generated by the kind of personal characteristics just described is put to use, a wide variety of interesting things happen. For one thing, sick churches become healthy churches. And healthy churches, like healthy people, exhibit certain vital signs. If the church is the Body of Christ, then there is some biblical justification in taking a rather clinical approach to analyzing the health of a church.

Human vital signs include pulse, respiration, blood pressure and temperature. If my temperature registers 98.6 degrees, I know it is a sign of health. And I know this is so because medical researchers have taken the temperatures of enough healthy people to determine "normal temperature." Enough data has since been accumulated by medical science so that diagnosis of health or illness is, in many cases, rather routine.

But what then are the vital signs of a healthy church?

Here are seven such indicators of ecclesiastical good health:

1. *The pastor.* What kind of a role must the pastor play if the church is to grow?

2. *The people of the church.* Is it possible for a church to grow if it has a perfect kind of pastor, but the wrong kind of people? How can the wrong kind of people become the right kind of people?

3. *Church size.* How big does a church need to be in order to be healthy and growing?

4. *Structure and functions.* How can a church be so structured that all of its primary functions are operating at peak efficiency?

5. *Homogeneous unit.* Is it important that a church be composed of basically one kind of people, or should it be a mixture of a variety of individuals—the wider the better?

6. *Methods.* What kinds of methods have proved to be effective instruments for evangelism in America today?

7. *Priorities.* How can the several good things that churches ought to do be prioritized according to biblical principles and effectiveness for growth?

But before we zero in for a closer look at these three vital signs we need first to ask one more question: Is the whole philosophy of church growth which causes us to ask all these questions pleasing to God?

Let's answer that last question first, shall we?

STUDY QUESTIONS

1. What did you learn from the examples of growing churches given in the text? Do you agree that there is no one method or one place where the church can grow? What method does your church use?

2. What do you think about the set of personal qualities that are outlined by the author concerning church growth leaders? Do you feel that your pastor has these qualities? If so, which ones are the most significant towards the growth of your church?
3. What are the author's vital signs for church growth? Again, do you feel that your church has these? If so, which ones are functioning to the full benefit of the church?

Chapter 2

WHAT IS CHURCH GROWTH ALL ABOUT?

At one time—before I met him—I thought Donald McGavran was an outright quack. What I had read in his *Church Growth Bulletin* (now *Global Church Growth*) was totally different from what I had learned previously. So I had a hard time understanding why my alma mater, Fuller Theological Seminary, invited *that* man to set up its new School of World Mission back in 1965.

Why? I had been turned off by McGavran's terminology!

Such terms as *scientific principles, new philosophy, accountability, theoreticians, practitioners,* and *professionals in the field* are uncommon vocabulary in most discussions of the Lord's work. And this unfamiliar language of the Church Growth Movement still raises questions in the minds of many dedicated Christian people.

Is this church growth approach really spiritual or might it be carnal?

Is there anything in God's Word that tells us we need to be "scientific" in bringing people to Christ?

Is there not a danger that sociology and computers may subtly take the place of the Holy Spirit?

In a word, does all this please God?

I know these questions are real because I was asking them myself when I first came, during my second missionary furlough from Bolivia, to study at Fuller under McGavran. Frankly, I entered his program in 1967 as a skeptic. But I emerged an enlightened person.

I had sipped from the fountainhead of what was to become a major stream of influence on worldwide Christianity. Lyle E. Schaller says that the Church Growth Movement was "the most influential development of the 1970s" on the American religious scene.

If I were not convinced that the church growth approach is true to God's Word and pleasing to Him, I personally would have no part of it. But at the same time I realize that there are some very good people who have tried it and don't like it. Never for a moment would I say that, because they reject church growth thinking, they are thereby displeasing God.

I may—and do—use my powers of persuasion to "enlighten" them, but all along I realize deep down that God may well be able to use them better outside of the framework of church growth philosophy than within. And blessings on them! I believe firmly in Christian liberty—maximum freedom for each Christian to find the leading of the Holy Spirit for his or her life and to minister accordingly.

But what of us who have chosen to embrace the church growth school of thought? Are we ourselves on firm biblical ground?

BIBLICAL ROOTS OF CHURCH GROWTH

The overall purpose of God for the unsaved people of the world is basic to New Testament Christianity and also to church growth. "For the Son of Man has come to seek and to save that which was lost," says Jesus Himself (Luke 19:10). The Lord is longsuffering, Peter adds, "not willing that any should perish but that all should come to repentance" (2 Pet. 3:9).

If these two verses were just isolated proof texts, they might not be sufficient to establish the premise for a major movement. But they are not. The God we see in the Bible is a seeking and a finding God.

Immediately after Adam and Eve ate the forbidden fruit and fell into sin, God called out to Adam in the garden, "Where are you?" (Gen. 3:9). Ever since then, He has actively been seeking people separated from Him by sin. He was so serious about it that He finally sent "His only begotten Son, that whoever believes in Him should not perish but have everlasting life" (John 3:16).

The provision God has made for bringing lost people to Himself is the gospel. This is the good news that Jesus commanded to be preached to every creature (see Mark 16:15). It is the gospel that Paul preached in power to the Thessalonians (see 1 Thess. 1:5) and that turned them "to God from idols to serve the living and true God" (1 Thess. 1:9). The difference between those who perish and those who are saved is their response to the gospel. Thus, it is crucial that all lost people in the world hear the gospel and hear it in such a way that they will repent of their sins and place their trust and commitment in Christ as their Lord.

For reasons impossible to understand fully, God has not chosen to make the gospel known all by Himself. No question that He could do it if He wanted to. But instead He has chosen to use Christian people to do the job.

"Whoever calls upon the name of the Lord shall be saved," the Bible says. But then it goes on to add, "How then shall they call on Him in whom they have not believed? And how shall they believe in Him of whom they have not heard? And how shall they hear without a preacher?" (Rom. 10:13-14).

The answer is obvious. There is no way to hear the message of God's love without a preacher. This implies that we human beings have a tremendously important responsibility in the execution of God's plan for the world. We may wish we didn't have to shoulder so much responsibility, but we cannot shirk it if we are serious about calling Jesus "Lord."

The New Testament frequently reminds us that we are "stewards of God." In biblical times, the steward was the person placed in charge of the affairs of the master. If the steward goofed, the master lost out, but the steward also paid the price (see Matt. 25:26-29).

The Bible clearly says that "it is required in stewards that one be found faithful" (1 Cor. 4:2). Faithful stewardship involves using all possible resources in accomplishing the will of the master. When this is done successfully, the steward is called good and *faithful* (Matt. 25:21, italics added).

Paul considered himself a "steward of the mysteries of God" (1 Cor. 4:1). He was entrusted with the *gospel*, even as we are. And Christians whose ministry is guided by a church growth philosophy take this stewardship very seriously.

The Master wants lost men and women found and saved. He expects His stewards to accomplish this objective and provides them with an all-important resource for doing it, namely the Holy Spirit. Jesus' disciples were told to tarry in Jerusalem "until you are endued with power from on high" (Luke 24:49).

The disciples waited and prayed. But once they were endued, they didn't wait anymore. They exploded into action on the day of Pentecost, and church growth began right then and there. Their numbers grew from 120 to

3,120 in one day, and every day after that it grew some more (see Acts 2:47).

The Spirit-filled steward is expected to use all available resources to serve the Master: time, money, and energy. And God wants it all used for His glory. Ironically, however, some conscientious Christians who are faithful stewards of their time and money are shy about using energy, particularly mental energy.

Without saying it in so many words, these Christians tend to think that the more people are filled with the Holy Spirit the less they have to use their minds. So, for them, the converse is also true: the more people use their minds, the less spiritual they are. Anyone thinking like this usually has real problems in accepting the church growth point of view.

God delights to "guide [us] with [His] eye." We are not to be like "the horse or like the mule, which have no understanding" (Ps. 32:8-9). The difference between humans and animals is that God made humans in His own image with minds that are rational. That's why Jesus was able to tell His followers that they were to love the Lord with all their *minds* as well as with their other faculties (Matt. 22:37).

SCIENCE IN GOD'S SERVICE

Using the mind well to understand, plan, and implement a specific task brings science into the picture. If the book of Acts tells us anything, it tells us that the task God has entrusted to us as His stewards is to share the good news of the gospel with every person who is not yet a Christian, introduce that person to Jesus Christ, and bring him or her into active fellowship with other Christians in the church.

God wants Christians to be multiplied and He wants churches to be multiplied. The task is tremendous and more complex than some might think. Sometimes God's work is well done, but sometimes it is badly bungled.

What makes the difference?

I recently heard a veteran missionary discuss this problem. He pointed out that in the old days in China some missionaries were doing a great job of evangelizing and planting new churches across the hills and plains of China. But others tried and tried and didn't succeed. He said that to them the answer for failure was invariably the same: "Go to Keswick."

It was assumed that all problems were ultimately spiritual. If only Christian workers could get closer to the Lord, if they could deepen their prayer life, if they studied the Word harder, if they "let go and let God"—well, then God would bless and they would become successful church planters.

The only thing wrong with this theory, the missionary went on to say, was that it rarely worked in practice. More often than not this approach compounded an already existing guilt complex and wrought disastrous results. It either heightened the sense of failure so that the worker returned home in discouragement or so hardened the conscience of the person that he or she no longer worried about whether they prompted any results or not.

Theological principles were even developed to explain failure away. "Leave the results to God" is yet a frequently used phrase. With this slogan the worker could finish out a difficult and sacrificial missionary career with very little fruit and never be concerned at all about whether a better job might have been done if more appropriate methods had been used.

I am altogether in favor of the kind of spiritual growth that takes place at Keswick or in any other situation where a person meets God in a special way. Meeting God on a regular basis is the highest priority in the life of a successful Christian worker. But to imagine that harvesters going into the whitened fields and coming out with empty arms at the end of the day is most likely a "spiritual problem" is, in my opinion, a somewhat simplistic approach. It is like hoping against hope that an automobile will fly if you just polish it enough and put high enough octane gasoline into the tank. No, to make an automobile fly will require many more complex changes.

The scientific aspect of church growth is vitally interested in understanding and describing all the factors which enter into cases of failure and success in evangelistic efforts. One of the factors, of course, is spiritual, but there are many more which also require explanation.

What Is Science All About?

Many do not understand exactly what science is all about. Science is nothing more than an attempt to explain certain phenomena in a reasonable and systematic way. Natural science tries to explain, for example, the organic composition of fossils or how an egg and sperm produce a fetus, what causes an eclipse of the moon, and many other things. Social science tries to explain such phenomena as why women in our culture marry men like their fathers, why some Africans intentionally scar their faces, why the suicide rate is high among some groups and low among others, and similar phenomena.

Church growth science follows suit. It tries to explain, in a reasonable and systematic way, why some churches grow and others decline, why some Christians are able to bring their friends to Christ and into church membership and others are not, or what are the symptoms of a terminal illness in a church.

The best of scientists in any field readily admit that all scientific knowledge is tentative. No scientific theories are ever proven, they just gain credibility and usefulness to the degree they are not yet *falsified*.

Scientists are always looking for better ways to explain the phenomena they study. For hundreds of years, for example, Ptolemy's theory of the universe was the best available scientific explanation of why the sun rises in the morning and sets in the evening. Then Copernicus offered a better theory which falsified Ptolemy's theory and has been useful ever since.

The germ theory of disease is a very useful one, but few believe that it is a totally adequate explanation of why some people get sick and some stay healthy. Newton's theories still explain many physical phenomena, but when matter and energy are shown to be interchangeable, they are no longer adequate. The reason Einstein became so famous is that his theory of relativity was able to explain many phenomena that had baffled scientists for centuries.

One of the great values of scientific theory is that as well as explaining the past they are useful in predicting the future. They help us know when a hurricane is approaching, what will happen to certain crops if lime and super-phosphate are added to the soil, whether a deep hole in a certain location is likely to strike oil, and many other things.

In no case, however, does science explain all. The world is still waiting for more useful explanations for the occurrence of earthquakes, for the origin of cancer cells or for extrasensory perception.

Church Growth as a Science

All science ultimately has its origin in God. Scientific theories simply help us understand God's creation better. Yet for some reason or other, a scientific approach has not been used widely among Christians for understanding God's work in the world with more precision. But church growth intends to do just that.

As a matter of curiosity, only one of the ten resident members on the faculty of the Fuller School of World Mission—where church growth theory has been generated to date—has a doctorate in theology as such. Faculty members come from such academic fields as civil engineering, education, social ethics, chemistry, linguistics, agriculture, and anthropology where scientific methodology is a prominent part of the training. Of course, each one has done basic graduate work in theology, but this is combined with a scientific approach not usually stressed in either theological seminaries or liberal arts colleges. The result is a new, and presumably useful, way of looking at what God is doing in the world.

Church growth science provides a new frame of reference from which to interpret old phenomena. Even though it claims no absolute "laws," the theories that emerge do sensitize us to see things that we never would have seen otherwise. It provides a new language, new labels, and new models for increasing our effectiveness as God's stewards.

Church growth as a science helps us maximize the use of energy and other resources for God's greater glory. It enables us to detect errors and correct them before they do too much damage.

Lack of church growth is a serious disease, but in most cases it is a curable one. The cure, however, is often not simple. It frequently requires as careful a diagnosis and therapy as a tumor on the ovary or a coronary thrombosis. One of the central tasks of the church growth school is (1) to develop scientific techniques of diagnostic research for ailing churches and (2) to design instruments to be used in the kind of therapy which will restore normal church health.

Just as in medicine, it takes specialized and professional training to use these new tools well. Sometimes a stomachache can be cured at home. But when Pepto-Bismol and Alka-2 fail, most people decide to seek the advice of a professional. This has not been true in our churches to any great extent, because few such professionals are available. But specialists are now being trained and equipped to give much more than superficial answers to the question, "Why isn't my church growing?" The premier training program for church growth consultants is the Diagnosis with Impact course offered by Carl F. George, director of the Charles E. Fuller Institute of Evangelism and Church Growth (Box 91990, Pasadena, CA 91109-1990).

HOW CAN A CHURCH GROW?

How to correct stagnation and decline in the church has become a high priority concern across the board in the America of the 1980s. More and more, as I travel across the country, I hear concerned laymen, pastors and denominational executives asking the same question: "What can we do to make our church grow?"

In the process of searching for answers to that question, I will be the first to admit that I am not nor have I ever been the pastor of a healthy, growing church. My self-identity is more that of an objective, scientific researcher. As a theoretician I have some disadvantages, but also some advantages.

It may not be obvious at first, but it is a fact that many pastors of growing churches have only vague insights into the reasons why their churches are growing. They have difficulty in seeing the forest for the trees. For example, I sometimes recommend a particular book describing the growth of one very large and very prominent church in America. In it the pastor of that church writes ten chapters, each one describing what he perceives to be one of the major reasons why his church is growing. But when my students—who are themselves pastors—write reviews of the book, they frequently comment that they still don't know why this church grows. Most of the ten reasons, they say, could also be used to describe many shrinking churches they know of.

McGavran, for example, tells of interviewing one pastor of a growing church who gave as the principal reason for its growth: "We preach the Bible as the Word of God and are faithful to it." Then McGavran asked the pastor of the church across the street from it why he thought his church had *not* grown for the last ten years. The answer: "We preach the Bible as the Word of God and are faithful to it."

The application is obvious.

Sometimes talking to pastors of growing churches reminds me of reading the stories of people who live to be a hundred. Particularly in a small town, the local newspaper will frequently interview any citizen who celebrates his or her hundredth birthday. Invariably one of the questions is, "What did you do to live so long?"

One person will say, "I lived a clean life, never drank and never smoked." But in the next town the centenarian will say, "The only thing that has kept me going this long has been a pint of whiskey a day and a box of cigars a week!"

Few people of that age know with any kind of accuracy why they have lived that long because they have not been trained to think scientifically about their life spans. Likewise, most pastors have not been trained to think scientifically. Some pastors do, however, have an excellent grasp on the growth dynamics of their church and are able to communicate them to others. I immediately think of my friends Robert Schuller and Richard Warren in this respect. There are not many like them.

Yet the vital signs of healthy churches are there, and somehow they need to be described in ways that are both intrinsically accurate and helpful to others. The person who does this must study a large number of churches across the board, not just the one he or she is directly involved in.

One of my professional responsibilities is to do this kind of research. Over the past ten years, I have visited scores of churches and interviewed hundreds of pastors. I have also read countless articles and books and graded hundreds of term papers analyzing the growth of churches.

In describing the seven vital signs of healthy churches as I have perceived them, I do not claim finality in my conclusions. Church growth is still a young science and new developments are breaking all the time. Yet it is encouraging to know that over the eight years that the seven vital signs have been tested, they have held up well. With few exceptions, church leaders have found them helpful in answering the question: Why do some churches grow while others do not?

If your church is not growing and you would like it to grow, it will require prayer, study, hard work and—above all—faith.

So let's begin at the beginning—with faith!

STUDY QUESTIONS

1. What do you think about the author's biblical stand concerning church growth? Do you believe that it is profitable for scientists to work with church growth? Do you believe that the Bible teaches the practicality of using our minds and measuring what God is doing in the world?

2. Do you agree that a pastor could have a growing church and still not be able to explain why the church grows without some sort of scientific measurement? Why?

Chapter 3

IS YOUR FAITH BIG ENOUGH?

An essential ingredient in all Christian work is faith. The Bible tells us point-blank that "without faith it is impossible to please [God]" (Heb. 11:6).

FAITH ON DISPLAY

In the mid 1970s, Raymond Ortlund then pastor of Lake Avenue Congregational Church, Pasadena, California printed this bold statement in his church bulletin:

There are over one million people living within 20 minutes' drive of Lake Avenue Church. When the freeway is completed the number will double. Most of these do not know Christ. We must share some of the responsibility to reach them for Christ. Some of them would not be open to us at all. But I estimate there are 50,000 who would respond to us and our style of ministry.

One of my dreams is that by 1990 (15 years from now) at least 5,000 would be worshipping God here every Sunday morning. That means we must prayerfully prepare ourselves, our ministry, our facilities for these precious people.

I also pray that we will begin several new congregations. I pray that we can minister to other churches and missions what God has taught us.

What a tragedy if we let money or glass, steel or mortar hinder our winning these lost to Christ and having a broad ministry for Him together.

I am asking that you think about this. Commit yourself to Christ and to one another for this glorious mission. Nice, decent people will never make it. Only those who are totally given to Christ and to His Body of believers will do this kind of frontline work.

Fresh commitment to Christ is first, but after that we love and sharpen each other for growth together. Then God, who calls the signals, will tell us "when" for each step ahead.

God bless you. Let's go for God!

Ortlund's statement was tremendously significant because he looked ahead to 1990 and saw his own church attendance at five thousand—more than double the church attendance at that time. He also envisioned the start of new churches, like his in the area, and new growth to stagnant churches—all as a result of his ministry.

All this is a formidable public display of *faith*. According to Hebrews 11:1, "Faith is the substance of things hoped for, the evidence of things not seen." Because Pastor Ortlund, through the eyes of faith, could see five thousand people praising God on the Lake Avenue Church campus, he could realistically face such things as how much money, glass, steel, and mortar it would take. This is the kind of attitude that pleases our Lord.

And God blesses it. One of the indications that Ray

Ortlund's vision had come from God is the fact that his successor, Pastor Paul Cedar, has received a similar vision for the church and continues to provide strong, quality leadership for growth.

Jesus and Faith

Jesus, time after time, taught His disciples the necessity of exercising faith. Matthew tells the story of a man who had a son who was demonized. Jesus' disciples tried to cure him, but they failed. Then Jesus cast the demon out and the child was cured instantly.

Afterward, the disciples asked why He could do it while they could not. "Because of your unbelief," Jesus said. "If you have faith as a mustard seed, . . . nothing will be impossible for you" (Matt. 17:20).

On another occasion Peter decided that if Jesus could walk on water, so could he. He started out to do it and it worked! But soon he lost his nerve and started to sink. What were Jesus' words of rebuke? "O you of little faith" (Matt. 14:31).

As Jesus looks over His present-day disciples, particularly those whom He is holding responsible as stewards of the resources that should be used for church growth, He must frequently say, "O you of little faith."

The Indispensable Condition

Without faith it is impossible to please God. Likewise without faith it is very difficult for churches to grow. If Christian people do not look ahead and by faith see their church growing, it in all probability will not grow well.

Faith involves setting goals in terms of things hoped for and things unseen. Or, as Edward Dayton says, "Every goal is a statement of faith." So a goal of five thousand by 1990 is a direct and intentional exercise of faith.

Remember, *the indispensable condition for a growing*

church is that it wants to grow. This does not mean, of course, that a church will grow by just wanting to. But if it doesn't want to grow, it will not grow. And if it is a growing church, it wants to grow. Wanting to grow and planning for growth is simply one tangible way of applying biblical faith.

It is a fact that some Christians do not want their church to grow. They are unimpressed by biblical and theological arguments for church growth. Somehow they have learned to rationalize their lethargy toward winning the lost to Christ, although with their lips they would deny that they are lethargic.

These believers have designed what Donald McGavran calls a "remnant theology," and they take a certain satisfaction in being a minority despised by unbelievers. They consider their unattractiveness a virtue and enjoy being described as "separate from the world." They write books with titles such as *Church Growth Is Not the Point.*

EXERCISE OF FAITH

The Pastor

The exercise of faith for church growth must come on two levels. First, the pastor must want the church to grow. The most formidable obstacle to growth that I know of is a pastor who thinks negatively and who is pessimistic about growth opportunities in the community. Such a pastor generally feels that the basic task of the church is to care for those sheep already in the fold rather than to concentrate on winning lost sheep and constantly incorporating new ones into the flock.

It is true that some ministers simply are not equipped psychologically to handle a church larger than a one-person operation. One minister is usually adequate for a church of one or two hundred members. When the church is below that level, that kind of a pastor may work hard for growth and perhaps attain it. But if something isn't changed, that person will almost automatically limit the growth.

When the church reaches a certain point, however, and when some begin suggesting that the staff might need to be increased, a threat arises and the pastor may begin—without publishing it in the bulletin—to plan for zero growth. And it is altogether possible that this may be done unconsciously without either the pastor or the lay leaders really understanding what is taking place in their church. They are puzzled why the church never seems to break through the 150 to 250 size.

It is a fact of life that some pastors are much better suited for small churches than for large ones. I want to go on record as affirming the valuable role which small churches and small church pastors play in the Kingdom of God. Eighty percent of American churches are two hundred and under and generally considered in the small-church category. Books such as Carl Dudley's *Making the Small Church Effective* (Abingdon) are extremely useful for such situations. This book has a different focus, however. It is addressed to pastors and lay leaders who feel that it is God's will for them to break what is called the "two hundred barrier" and enjoy continuous growth. My first piece of advice for them is to exercise faith and believe that God wants the church to grow.

The Laity

The second level on which faith must be exercised for church growth is with the people of the church. The lay leaders in particular must want their church to grow. If they do not, they can effectively and almost effortlessly prevent it.

One of the chief causes for a negative attitude on the

part of laypeople is that the congregation has become almost like an extended family. They have grown to know and love each other so much that they feel extremely uncomfortable when an outsider penetrates their inner circle. Again this is often unconscious, but outsiders soon get the message that they are not fully welcome and they will not stay around the church very long under those conditions.

There are other causes as well. An undue stress on Christian perfection can turn a congregation into spiritual navel-gazers who are so pleased with their own heroic attainments that they have little tolerance for newer Christians who are not as polished. They are somewhat like middle-aged couples who detest the thought of changing diapers and all that goes with having children so they carefully practice birth control to avoid that possibility.

Again, a congregation full of bickering and backbiting also becomes very self-centered. So much energy is spent on trying to hold the internal pieces together and to survive that little attention is given to winning the lost. Even if some were won, they would not find there an atmosphere for healthy Christian growth and would likely shop around for a more satisfying church home. Worse yet, they might end up being "spiritual orphans."

FAITH PLUS WORKS

But suppose that the pastor and the lay leaders all do want the church to grow. It has already been mentioned that this in itself is not enough to assure growth. The faith might be there, but as the Epistle of James asserts, "faith without works is dead" (Jas. 2:20). In that light then, I expand my former statement to say that the *indispensable condition for a growing church is that it wants to grow and is willing to pay the price for growth.*

Robert Schuller warns that "if you fail to plan you plan

to fail." Growth happens only in churches that plan for growth. And an essential part of planning includes anticipating the cost.

Church growth costs time. A church of two thousand is ever so much more demanding than a church of two hundred. It costs energy. It might mean two or three sermons on a Sunday morning rather than one. It means more and longer board meetings. It means planning sessions and long-range task forces.

And it costs money. True, the new members will help pay the bills, but the key decisions for growth must be taken even before new people come into the picture, and thus they require a considerable measure of faith.

This very practical corollary of faith must not be slighted or overlooked. It is easy to do. It is easy to assume that if through the teaching of the Word the congregation develops high enough levels of faith, love, hope, prayer, and worship, then growth will come spontaneously.

Spontaneous growth is a pleasant dream. Sometimes it happens, but not very frequently. Planning for growth and agreeing to pay the price for growth is much more realistic. Even growing churches which claim spontaneous growth, upon analysis, will usually reveal a significant degree of planning below the surface.

Donald Hamman, former pastor of the Medinah (Illinois) Baptist Church, is well aware of growth dynamics. He and his people wanted to grow so much that they described their church as the "church on the grow."

In a dramatic challenge for growth to his church in 1970, Hamman—sounding very much like Hebrews 11:1—reminded his people that moving forward would be a "venture into the unknown." He realistically predicted many "stumbles and mistakes" as they moved ahead together, but he was not afraid of risk. He had faith in

God's power to carry them.

"But such progress does not come by chance," Hamman said. "It comes by setting primary goals and then by planning and programming to meet those goals."

Planned growth paid top dividends in the Medinah Baptist Church. In ten years from the early 1960s to the early 1970s, when many churches in America were on the decline, the church grew from eighty-five to three hundred members with a Sunday morning attendance of over a thousand.

A decadal growth rate of upwards of 250 percent is excellent for any church in any decade. Many churches would feel encouraged if they were growing at half or even one quarter that rate.

Goals for Growth

Hamman would agree with Edward Dayton that "every goal is a statement of faith." Churches that really want to grow will set bold goals for growth.

The fact that relatively few churches do set goals is a sign that they are not as serious about wanting to grow as they say they are. They remind me of some of my overweight friends who feel very self-conscious about their size. These people are always talking about getting more exercise and going on a diet, but year after year they stay about the same. In my understanding, their actions prove they don't really *want* to lose weight, regardless of what they say.

Likewise, many evangelical churches tell everyone they want to grow, but they stay about the same year after year. Why? They fail to set bold goals and then do whatever is necessary to attain them.

Timidity Causes Failure

The chief deterrent to creative and courageous goal

setting on the part of church leadership is timidity. Not to have goals, of course, is an extremely comfortable situation since with no goals it is impossible to fail.

No one wants to fail, and many have convinced themselves that failure can be avoided by aiming at nothing. It has rarely occurred to these timid souls that while their system disallows failure, it also disallows success.

So some who want to report success, but who fear risk, have developed a very useful alternative technique of *talking* about their goals. Their goals are whatever they happen to be doing at the time.

This method is fail-safe. It is like shooting a bullet into the wall, then drawing the target around the bullet hole.

Although this method of goal-setting can and does fool some people, it does not fool the Lord for one moment. He sees such people as adding to the already swollen number of "you of little faith."

Taking a risk is part and parcel of exercising faith. This is clear in the parable of the talents, or thousands of dollars as *The Living Bible* has it. Notice that the businessman in the parable who gave his employees $5,000, $2,000 and $1,000 to invest respectively expected a high return on his investment.

The two "good and faithful servants" made a 100 percent return on the investment. Evidently this return was considerably above what the current rate of bank interest was, since the businessman told the "wicked and slothful servant" that the least he could have done with his money was put it in the bank (see Matt. 25:27, *TLB*). But, as every businessman knows, a high return invariably involves a high risk.

God wants us to be bold. He wants us to take risks for Him. He expects a high return from His stewards.

The steward who buried his money had no goal except to avoid failure. He admitted, "I was afraid" (Matt. 25:25,

TLB). And what did his timidity gain him?

Failure!

Lack of faith is always and inexorably self-defeating.

POSSIBILITY THINKING

No one that I know is more eloquent in exposing lack of faith on the part of church leaders than Pastor Robert Schuller of the Crystal Cathedral. Faith is not just theory to him. He has built it into his very life-style.

In my judgment a staunch attitude of faith has been the basic catalyst for the growth rate of over 500 percent per decade that the Garden Grove Community Church maintained over its first twenty years of existence. Its membership of ten thousand is ample evidence that hard at work there are some "good and faithful servants."

The point I want to make is that Pastor Schuller himself had to overcome a deep fear of failure in order to begin setting growth-stimulating goals. It happened when he fixed his attention on a slogan written across the top of a wall calendar: "I'd rather attempt to do something great and fail than attempt to do nothing and succeed." He allowed God to burn this concept into his soul, and it became one of the generating forces that produced his well-known philosophy of "possibility thinking."

Possibility thinking boils down basically to a synonym of what the Bible calls "faith." Schuller's definition of possibility thinking is "the maximum utilization of the God-given powers of imagination exercised in dreaming up possible ways by which a desired objective can be attained." He is convinced that "the greatest power in the world is the power of possibility thinking."

"If your dream is from God," he adds, "then you need only to exercise this miracle-working power, and you can reach the seemingly unattainable goal!" Jesus continually tried to get this idea over to His disciples when He said,

"If you have faith as a mustard seed . . . " (Matt. 17:20).

Pastor Thomas Ray of Central Baptist Temple, Huntington Beach, California is a possibility thinker. And his church is an example of outstanding growth. A former car salesman, Ray may well have learned the principles of goal-setting in the secular world.

God has consistently directed Ray into small, static churches where an infusion of possibility thinking is much needed. He first went into the Crestview Baptist Church in Irving, Texas where twenty-five people were still meeting in a home. Within five years Sunday School attendance had topped six hundred.

Then he was called to Central Baptist Temple. It was a struggling church of fifty people and deep in debt. Before long the average attendance on Sunday was over fourteen hundred.

How did it happen? It is a long story, but the climate was set in Pastor Ray's very first sermon of his ministry in Huntington Beach. He gathered his fifty members together and told them, "Nothing can keep us from growing, nothing!"

This was possibility thinking in action. But it has not ceased. Even though he was soon speaking to standing-room-only crowds, Pastor Ray still boldly proclaimed, "We've got to double our attendance, double our buses, double our facilities, double our staff; but it will cost money—we've all got to double our giving!"

Because it is so biblical, I remain convinced that without faith, it is impossible for churches to grow. Empirical evidence also validates the absolute necessity of faith or whatever else you want to call it—possibility thinking or goal-setting—as a prerequisite for church growth.

In other words, *the indispensable condition for a growing church is that it wants to grow and is willing to pay the price for growth.*

STUDY QUESTIONS

1. After reading this chapter, do you have a new perspective of faith as it relates to church growth? What are the two levels of faith discussed by the author? How could this relate to your responsibilities in your own church?
2. Is your church willing to grow and pay the price? If so, how could you measure your church's willingness? Illustrate.
3. The author is convinced that faith is an absolute necessity for church growth. Do you agree? Discuss this as a group.

Chapter 4

PASTOR, DON'T BE AFRAID OF POWER!

In America, the primary catalytic factor for growth in a local church is the pastor. In every growing, dynamic church I have studied, I have found a key person whom God is using to make it happen.

You can check this out for yourself. Just take a book like *Great Churches of Today* or Elmer Towns' *America's Fastest Growing Churches* and note the examples given of growing churches in the U.S. today. Almost without exception, the churches cited in these books have grown under the leadership of one person in particular to whom God has given special gifts and who is using these gifts to lead the church into growth.

It is normal for pastors of growing churches to deny that they are primary keys to growth. For one thing, this is due to sincere Christian humility. These pastors are people of God. They are acutely aware of the dangers of pride and haughtiness. They have preached to their congregations that "pride cometh before a fall" and they do not want to fall. They want God to have the glory and

Jesus to be exalted. They are willing to decrease if Jesus can increase.

They also have profound respect for fellow ministers, many of whom are not experiencing growth at all in their churches. It is contrary to their sense of Christian graciousness to allow themselves to be placed in a position that might give the impression that they somehow think themselves superior to other ministers and thus become alienated from them.

Furthermore, pastors of growing churches know they are not doing it alone, and they want to be the first to make this plain. Many of them work with a loyal and competent staff, and everybody is aware of the essential contribution that each staff member is making toward the growth of the church. No pastor desires to take credit for what a staff colleague is doing. So the pastor will frequently say, "Don't think I am responsible for this; I am just one member of a fantastic team."

And again, a good pastor will want to give due credit to the laypeople. Where the pastor is the only staff member in smaller churches, if the small church is a growing church, the people in the congregation are invariably pulling their weight. They are working hard. And no church, large or small, can grow well unless this happens.

Most pastors, then, will be careful to make sure that the people of the congregation are well aware of their dependence on them, and they will remind them of it as often as possible. So as not to jeopardize the spiritual dynamic already at work among the people they will be very hesitant to accept public credit for the growth of the church.

It is true, then, that no pastor, regardless of how gifted, can make a church grow alone. The Body of Christ was not designed to function that way. From just the practical point of view, anyone could soon deduce that the only pastor who could possibly do all the work would be the pastor of a very small church. But if that small church is *growing* it soon will be a church too large for any one person to do all the work involved. The larger a church grows, the less a share of the total workload the pastor can assume.

DYNAMIC PASTORAL LEADERSHIP

Vital Sign Number One of a healthy, growing church is a pastor who is a possibility thinker and whose dynamic leadership has been used to catalyze the entire church into action for growth. Interestingly enough, the first ones to recognize this are usually the members of the congregation themselves.

As I visit growing church after growing church I try to get the pulse of the average person in the pew as far as his or her attitude toward the pastor is concerned. Invariably I find a high degree of love and esteem for their leader. As a matter of fact, this is often exaggerated to the extent that many members of a growing church will claim—and sincerely so—that their pastor is the best pastor in the whole world.

How I love to hear that! Sometimes just to test it, I hint at a mild criticism of the pastor and watch the church member rise to the defense. When this happens, I know by that attitude alone that I am in a healthy church.

I compare such feelings to those in a happy family where the husband thinks his wife is the world's greatest and where the kids think there is no one like their dad. We smile when we hear a young child challenge a friend by saying, "My dad can lick your dad!" I also smile when I hear an adult Christian say—in effect, "My pastor can lick your pastor!"

Any outside observer knows that such statements are not based on objective facts. But this is unimportant. The important thing in this case is the *feeling* of the person who is involved in the church as an insider. Strong pastors of strong churches have earned the fierce loyalty of their parishioners. The sheep love their shepherd.

A personal story here concerning my wife, Doris, and me will illustrate the point I am making about parishioner loyalty. One day, after I had received a very attractive offer for a position in a midwestern city, we played a game. By this time, of course, we had prayed about it and knew that God wanted us to stay in Pasadena, so the discussion took on a light tone.

We discussed the kids' schooling and how disruptive a move would be for them, but decided that they had moved many times before and could probably do it again. We thought of the cold winters and hot summers and the need for woolen clothing, fuel oil, and anti-freeze, but thought if we had adapted to the jungles and mountains of Bolivia we could adapt again. We love our Spanish colonial house, but realized deep down that it was just another material possession that could never stand in the way of doing the will of God. We are stimulated by the ethnic diversity in our integrated community and did not relish moving into a blah, WASP small town, but if worse came to worse, we could make the adjustment.

To this point we were having fun. Then all of a sudden Doris's expression became serious and her eyes misted. I knew instantly the game was over.

"There's one thing we wouldn't have if we moved there," she said in a somber tone of voice. "Our pastor wouldn't be there, and he is something I for one am not at all prepared to consider giving up! No church in that other city could compare to ours."

I have thought about that incident many times because it pointed up—in a way very close to home for me—one of the dynamics of a growing church. Lake Avenue Congregational Church is the eighth church we have joined since we were converted twenty-five years ago. Of the eight, it is the first *growing* church we have been associated with.

We did not decide to join the church years ago because of the pastor, although we were acquainted with him casually and had a good opinion of his ministry. We joined primarily because we thought our children would benefit from the youth program. What happened to us after we joined should happen to every Christian.

We felt welcome in the church, we felt enveloped with a genuine spirit of love and concern, we caught some of the excitement of growth and vitality, and in the midst of it all it gradually became evident to us that God was using one person above all others to make it happen—the pastor. Until Doris and I played our game, however, I had not realized how deep the feeling had become.

Pastoral Authority

The kind of love that people in growing churches have for their pastor carries with it some implications that are not always recognized at first. One of these is that the pastor ends up with a great deal of authority. This is not an authority that has been bestowed by ordination, erudition or job description. This is God-given authority that the pastor has earned through relationships.

I have observed this fact of church life in Baptist and Nazarene, Presbyterian and Pentecostal, and churches of many other denominations. I have seen it in large churches and small churches, black churches and white churches. The pattern follows in Florida, New England, Texas and Indiana. The pastor of a growing church is typically a strong authority figure and that authority has been earned through living relationships with the people.

This is very similar to what often happens in a family

situation. A father who loves his wife as Christ loved the church (Eph. 5:25) and who brings up his children in the nurture and admonition of the Lord (Eph. 6:4) often finds himself with a great deal of authority. His wife is willing to obey and fulfill his every wish and his children honor him and are in subjection.

Biblically, this is what a family ought to be like, and it is no mere coincidence that such a family situation is a prerequisite for church leadership in the Pastoral Epistles. A bishop, according to the Apostle Paul, must rule his own house well and have his children in subjection, "For if a man does not know how to rule his own house, how will he take care of the church of God?" (1 Tim. 3:5).

When the head of a family has earned such authority, it often amazes outsiders. "I don't see how he gets away with what he does," some will comment. Others may say, "That woman is nothing but a slave!" Or even stronger, "He's a tyrant!" Those who have not lived it have a hard time understanding it.

A parallel situation exists in churches with pastors who have earned strong authority in the church. The church is—or should be—like a family. Frequently I have heard outsiders, particularly from non-growing churches, criticize the larger churches by saying something like: "They wouldn't be anywhere if it weren't for that one person."

"What will they do when they don't have Jack Hyles anymore?"

"What will happen to the church when Schuller is gone?"

"If Jim Kennedy were to leave, the church would collapse!"

Because they are repeated so frequently, such statements must have some significance for those who use them. Yet members of these growing churches with wonderful pastors do not think this way themselves anymore than most women who have wonderful husbands think they are bad off now because when their husbands die, life will not be the same for them again. It is all too true, but it is not immediately important. The fact of the matter is that Hammond First Baptist *does* have Jack Hyles, the Crystal Cathedral *does* have Robert Schuller, Coral Ridge Presbyterian *does* have James Kennedy, and in these and numerous other churches like them unsaved people are being brought to Christ and into an exciting family of God!

Of course, the next generation will have to be saved too, but it is not healthy for a church to spend too much time worrying about the next generation any more than it is healthy for a woman to spend too much time thinking about whom she will marry if her husband dies and leaves her a widow. The only generation any church is responsible for winning is this generation. The ripened harvest is ripe today, and the most important thing a church can do is what it is doing *now.*

Pastoral Longevity

One of the reasons why growing churches do not have to spend much time worrying about what will happen when their pastor goes is that a substantial number of pastors of growing churches have considered their particular parish to be a lifetime calling. They are not looking around for greener pastures.

Such pastors are excited about what they are doing and they are fulfilled in their ministry. They love the people as much as the people love them. They do not regularly ask themselves, "Could it be that my ministry here is ending?" Pastors of growing churches are generally characterized by longevity in the ministry.

This principle of longevity does not apply only to the senior minister in a multiple staff church. In the healthiest situation it applies to the staff as well. Not all pastors have the gifts necessary to lead a church into prolonged growth. Many, by nature, are suited better for a subordinate role, and they are happy to work under a compatible senior minister their whole lives. Strong staffs are built on this kind of person.

Beware of the person who accepts a staff position only as a stepping stone to a higher status or a larger church. Look for a minister of Christian education for whom Christian education is a lifetime area of specialization. Look for a youth minister who will be as capable of working with youth at age forty-five and not only at age twenty-five. Find a minister of visitation who will not get restless if he is not invited to take the pulpit frequently.

If a staff is built on the basis of spiritual gifts and calling to each particular position, it will be a strong one. Staff members under those circumstances will not tend to be jealous of or resent the authority of the senior pastor. In many social situations, including churches, there is usually room for only one person at the top. If all who are involved respect this truth and are content with their present situation, maximum progress can be made.

Pastoral Leadership

Pastoral authority, earned through a loving relationship with the family of God, is thus an important ingredient for growth. To some it might appear as dictatorship or totalitarianism, but it is not. It is the recognition and exercise of God-given spiritual gifts in the Body of Christ. I have expanded on this principle in my book, *Leading Your Church to Growth* (Regal).

Some congregational-type churches oppose strong pastoral leadership on principle. Congregationalism was developed along with American democracy, and strong pastoral authority seems undemocratic to some Christians. Where this feeling persists, it needs to be overcome if the church wants to move into a pattern of growth.

Pastor Donald Hamman of Medinah Baptist Church became strongly aware of this problem in a congregational-type church. In the period I am describing it had a membership of around three hundred, and is a church relatively easy to identify with in comparison with Schuller's ten thousand, Hyles's seventy-four thousand or Kennedy's three thousand.

Growth Rate Analysis

Before describing Pastor Hamman's leadership style, it would be well to know more about the church. In 1964, the church had eighty-five members. At the end of 1974, it had three hundred. But in this case, the communicant membership does not tell the whole story. It is much more helpful to use "composite membership" as the data base for analyzing church growth.

The composite membership factor was first introduced by Charles Mylander in 1975. Mylander found that membership statistics alone were not very useful in comparing the growth of four Friends churches in Orange County, California. So he experimented with several formulas and finally concluded that a combination of membership, worship attendance, and Sunday School attendance gave a much more accurate picture.

Composite membership is calculated by adding (1) the membership at the end of the year—however the particular church chooses to define membership; (2) the average worship attendance for the year—leave Christmas and Easter in, for they will usually be counterbalanced by the "summer slump"; and (3) the average Sunday School attendance—Sunday School enrollment is probably less realistic than attendance. Then divide the total by three to get the composite membership figure.

At the end of 1974 the membership of Medinah Baptist

was 300, the worship service averaged slightly over 1,000 and the Sunday School also was slightly over 1,000. This gives a composite membership of 767. In 1964 the composite membership was 198. Over that decade, then, the composite growth rate of the church was 287 percent.

Now, without a point of comparison, such a figure is meaningless. Is a 287 percent decadal growth rate good, bad, or indifferent? In other words, *how fast is fast growth*?

A rule of thumb established years ago by Donald McGavran states that *biological growth* should be calculated on the basis of 25 percent per decade. Biological growth occurs when the children of believers are raised in a Christian way, taught about Jesus, converted, and incorporated into the church membership.

It is obvious that the 25 percent figure would vary according to the population growth of the particular region in which the church is located, but much experimentation has shown that more precise calculations do not ultimately help the analysis. Use the 25 percent per decade as a starting point for thinking of church growth. In other words, if a church is growing at only 25 percent per decade, it is barely growing at all.

In the U.S.A. (other countries might differ), a decadal growth rate of 50 percent is not too bad. Not really healthy perhaps, but not unhealthy either. A church growing at 100 percent per decade is in pretty good shape. If it shows 200 percent, the church is newsworthy, and when the figure gets up around 300 percent the pastor better prepare to hold seminars to share the methods with others. For sure, he or she is doing something very significant.

So this gives us a handle to understand that the growth rate of 287 percent per decade in the Medinah Baptist Church is excellent. Before going on, however, notice that when analyzing the growth of a church, the bottom line should be expressed in *rates* of growth, not in absolute numbers. This method will soon deflate inflated member-ship statistics and keep everybody involved honest and out of the "numbers game." It also provides a uniform way of comparing otherwise differing churches across the board.

Medinah Baptist grew extremely well. It had many things going for it. It had a good location in a Chicago sub-urb, the population was growing, the congregation was devoted and hardworking. However, the leadership of Donald Hamman was the decisive factor. One observer describes him as "a capable, spiritual, intelligent, analyti-cal, industrious, loving leader with gifts of evangelist, pas-tor and teacher."

Dissolve Committees

On February 8, 1970, Hamman exercised his constitu-tional privilege of calling a special church business meet-ing. He knew intuitively that the church had reached a cru-cial point for its growth, so he prepared what he called a "Crossroads Message" for his people. In it, he laid his own future as a pastor of the church on the line.

With a Sunday morning attendance of 450, he felt that the church had begun to feel self-satisfied and was ready to settle with the status quo. Hamman's godly restless-ness would not tolerate such an attitude. In his message he demanded that the church push forward to new growth with the objective of "becoming the unquestioned Gospel-preaching evangelistic center in the entire metropolitan Chicago area."

Combined with this God-sized dream was an enviable touch of realism. Hamman felt that, like most churches he knew, Medinah Baptist was programmed and structured for mediocrity. "Our bulky bureaucracy of committees is a hindrance to action," he declared. He felt that committees were too often an excuse for busyness rather than vehicles for decisive planning. He described committee work as "much deliberation, considerable aggravation, unnecessary tensions and very little action!"

So he went on to reason with the congregation about his role as a leader. First he asked them if they really trusted him. Did they trust his doctrinal purity, his financial integrity, his moral uprightness, his unfeigned love of the brethren and his dedication to the work?

The congregation knew him well, and their answers to all the questions were positive. He had *earned* their love and respect.

Having established this, he then asked for a fresh mandate as their leader. "If you believe God has called me to pastor this church," he asked, "then will you follow me?"

He likened the total church to an army. This army has only one Commander-in-Chief, Jesus Christ. The local church is like a company with one company commander, the pastor, who gets orders from the Commander-in-Chief. The company commander has lieutenants and sergeants for consultation and implementation, but the final responsibility for decisions is that of the company commander, who must answer to the Commander-in-Chief.

In effect, Donald Hamman was saying to his congregation that Medinah Baptist had a great opportunity for growth ahead, but that if the church wanted to grow it had to streamline its decision-making process. It had to get rid of the bulky and cumbersome committee structure. It had to implement the principle underlying this whole chapter: *the pastor has the power in a growing church.*

The congregation bought Hamman's plan and made him company commander. In doing so, they voted out of existence fifteen standing committees! What happened afterward?

The church was growing well when all this took place in 1970, but it grew even better after restructuring. The growth rate for the five years preceding the "Crossroads Message" was 253 percent (projected to the decadal rate) and for the five years afterwards it went up to 325 percent. That figures down to an increase in the average annual rate from 13.4 percent to 15.6 percent.

Good progress!

Two other brief case studies reinforce this point that the pastor has the power in a growing church. Consider here the position of the pastor in two churches in Southern California which attract enormous congregations at Sunday morning worship: Melodyland Christian Center of Ahaheim (10,000) and Calvary Chapel of Costa Mesa (12,500).

Melodyland's constitution states that Pastor Ralph Wilkerson "shall be the executive head of the church and the president of the corporation . . . he shall be the spiritual overseer of the church and shall direct all its activities." According to researcher Henry Lord, this policy works out in practice. He says that Wilkerson "is the controlling power in this church . . . he works under the control of the Holy Spirit and so has his authority from God . . . He uses deacons as advisors and for legal purposes."

In Calvary Chapel, Pastor Chuck Smith is in charge of the church and holds himself accountable directly to the Lord. The constitution says, "The pastor shall be the president of the corporation and have the general supervision of the entire program and shall perform all necessary duties relating to such supervision."

THE ROUGH ROAD TO LEADERSHIP

As we have indicated earlier, the process of earning the love and trust of a congregation is far from an automatic one. Often it will bring the pastor who has a vision for growth up against a severe personal crisis experience. I have heard pastor after pastor tell of heartrending situations where their leadership was challenged and where it took all the courage and faith in God they could possibly muster to weather the storm.

In public I have heard W.A. Criswell of First Baptist Dallas tell of his crisis experience with his board of deacons. I have heard Robert Schuller tell of his desire to die of a heart attack so he could fail with honor when an obstinate consistory stood in the way of the vision God had given him for growth. I have heard several similar stories in private, some too intimate to relate.

Elmer Towns told me of one pastor who broke down in tears when he recalled his leadership crisis experience. Theological seminaries do not usually prepare young people for such crises, and I fear that too many ministers who are faced with them come out on the losing end and limp through the rest of their ministries, bruised and resigned to mediocrity.

This is not to say that a pastor continually at odds with the people will turn out to be a leader for church growth. The crisis experience I am talking about is not a regular pattern. It usually happens only once. As a result, some good members may leave the church disgruntled and bitter. That is regrettable, but it is part of the price that often needs to be paid.

The leader must be *the* leader. As Robert Schuller has said, "Let there be no dodging of this issue. Pastor? Do you hear me? You should be the spark plug. You should be the inspiring commander leading the troops up the hill!"

Maintain Your Authority

Pastors of growing churches who have earned their authority also know how to maintain it. They lead. They are out in front. But never too far in front. Anne Ortlund suggests in her book *Up with Worship* that sometimes the preacher needs to learn more from the people than they need to learn theology. "Listen to your dear flock," she pleads. "Get to know them deeply, their needs, their joys . . . *Scratch 'em where they itch.*"

It usually turns out that way. Pastors of growing churches may appear to outsiders to be dictators. But the people in the churches identify with their decisions. Almost as if they had a sixth sense, they know how to lead the church where the people want to go, and they also know how to catalyze the people so they themselves enter into the total work of the church enthusiastically and get the job done. In turn, the people trust the pastors.

Let's take a look next at how all this happens!

STUDY QUESTIONS

1. What are some of the personal characteristics of pastors with growing churches?
2. How do the people at the church see such a pastor? Do they see him differently than you see your pastor? If so, name some of the differences.
3. How fast should a church grow? How fast does your church grow?

Chapter 5

LIBERATE THE LAYPEOPLE!

If the first vital sign of a growing church is a pastor who is using God-given gifts to lead the church into growth, the second is a well-mobilized laity. One cannot function apart from the other any more than blood circulation and respiration can function apart from each other in the human body.

In a smaller church of up to two-hundred members the pastor can do all the work, and many do. But such a church will not be able to grow past that point without lay ministry.

Pastors of growing churches, whether they be large or small, know how to motivate their laypeople, how to create structures which permit them to be active and productive, and how to guide them into meaningful avenues of Christian service.

Activating laypeople for church growth has become more feasible in our day than at any other time in recent church history. This is due to what I like to call the "lay liberation" movement.

THE APPEARANCE OF LAY LIBERATION

Lay liberation began in the late 1960s with a general awakening throughout American churches of almost all stripes to the biblical teaching on spiritual gifts. As we look back from our present vantage point many of us wonder how it could possibly be that for so many years, and even centuries, God's people had such a low level of both understanding and practice in the area of spiritual gifts. It must have grieved God, as it did the Apostle Paul when he wrote to the Corinthians, "Now concerning spiritual gifts, brethren, I do not want you to be ignorant" (1 Cor. 12:1).

We have been so ignorant, and God has been so patient!

My own opinion is that the Pentecostal movement has played a key role in stimulating laymen's lib. Twenty years ago I studied under one of America's finest evangelical seminary faculties, but when I graduated I had been taught virtually nothing useful concerning spiritual gifts. I was ordained in an evangelical church, but no one asked me what my spiritual gifts were when I was examined by the ordination council. I joined an evangelical mission board that sent me to South America, but neither in the application form nor in the personal interviews was the matter of my spiritual gifts ever raised.

I would consider this almost unbelievable if I were not able to explain it at least to my own satisfaction. I now realize that my seminary professors, the ministers who ordained me and the mission executives were all still struggling to come to comfortable terms with the Pentecostal movement back in the early and mid-1950s. They were still debating whether Pentecostals were true Christians. I recall reading a book on false cults which contained chapters on Christian Science, Mormonism, *Pentecostalism,* Jehovah's Witnesses, and so forth.

Some people were saying that speaking in tongues was

produced by the devil himself. Many Christian leaders seemed to be spooked by reports of miraculous healings and prophecies. When the question came up in class in seminary we were usually told to read a book by Benjamin Warfield which argued that many of the biblical gifts were phased out after the church got rolling, and that we were not to look for them in our churches today.

But times have changed. Through the 1960s the charismatic movement began to trickle out of institutional Pentecostalism into many of the denominations that had previously opposed it. The leaders of the large Pentecostal denominations such as Assemblies of God and Church of the Foursquare Gospel developed rapport and then fellowship with their counterparts in other denominations. Pentecostalism gradually became respectable, and one of the many benefits for non-Pentecostals was a more relaxed attitude toward the biblical teaching on spiritual gifts.

By the mid-1960s the matter of spiritual gifts had become one of my own areas of high priority interest. I, myself, attempted to clarify issues in a book on First Corinthians, but I believe the real turning point to be the publication of *Body Life,* written by Pastor Ray Stedman of Peninsula Bible Church in Palo Alto, California. The unusual popularity of that book in 1972 is due largely to a receptive climate for spiritual gifts that already had been five years in the making.

Lay liberation had begun in force!

The subject of spiritual gifts has since become one of the hot items in theological seminaries. Recent graduates have been trained to avoid the clericalism of the past and to consider themselves "equippers" rather than old-fashioned parsons. Many consider their top priority is to get the laypeople of their churches active in the life of their church.

Pastor Lloyd Ogilvie of Hollywood Presbyterian

Church says, "We do not allow the people of the church to call those of us on the staff 'ministers.' We want every member of the church to consider himself or herself a minister of God." All these signs indicate that, more than ever before in recent memory, we live in an age where the layperson is a prominent factor in churches everywhere.

"Total Mobilization" Can Go Sour

As far as church growth is concerned, lay liberation has opened up fantastic new possibilities. If laypeople become excited about what they can do for God and for their church, the sky is the limit. But it is a fact of life that mere increased activity on the part of the laypeople in a church does not always help that church to grow.

Research has shown that some massive, well-organized, heavily financed efforts to achieve "total mobilization" of congregations for evangelism has hindered rather than helped church growth. Some of these efforts have reminded me of a boat with a big motor but a defective rudder. It has plenty of power, but fails to arrive at its destination.

It is no longer a mystery why this happens. Increased knowledge of spiritual gifts has identified the defects of unproductive efforts at "total mobilization." During the 1960s, one of the guiding philosophies of evangelism called the "Strachan theorem"—after Kenneth Strachan of the Latin American Mission—suggested that "the expansion of any movement is in direct proportion to its success in mobilizing its total membership in continuous propagation of its beliefs." In nation after nation, denomination after denomination, church after church, this was attempted for at least a decade. But in virtually no instance did it succeed in becoming (1) a total mobilization of church members for evangelistic work, (2) a continuous mobilization in cases where the initial enthusiasm was high, or, consequently,

(3) a contributing factor in helping churches to increase their previous rates of growth.

Why did such efforts fizzle? Certainly not because of advocating the mobilization of laity as a necessary factor for growth. No, the problem arises when everyone is expected to be a "continuous propagator." This is contrary to one of the major biblical teachings on spiritual gifts, namely, "If the whole body were an eye, where would be the hearing?" (1 Cor. 12:17). If everybody in the church is expected to be an evangelist, where are those with all the other spiritual gifts that are needed to make those with the gift of evangelist most effective?

Are Five Legs Better Than Two?

Think now in terms of the human body. Suppose our goal for the moment is to walk to a place a long distance away in the shortest period of time. Suppose we had the power to transpose one member of our body into another.

Would it make any sense to say we could walk faster with five legs than with two, so we will thus change our liver, our tongue, and one lung to legs? Of course not. With no liver, one hundred legs would not be able to operate at all. God has fashioned our physical bodies in perfect proportion so that all members work in harmony to help each other function as they should.

But this is exactly what the Bible says God has done with the Church, the Body of Christ. In each of the three major lists of spiritual gifts in the Bible, Romans 12, 1 Corinthians 12 and Ephesians 4, they are placed in the context of the Body of Christ. "God has set the members, each one of them, in the body just as He pleased" (1 Cor. 12:18). Every single believer has been fitted into the Body of Christ according to God's master plan, and has been given one or more spiritual gifts to fulfill that function properly.

There is nothing in the Bible to indicate that it is up to Christians to choose their spiritual gifts for themselves. The choice is up to God, and the first responsibility of every Christian is to discover which of the gifts God has given to him or her.

In the process, of course, it is natural that the person will also discover which of the gifts God has *not* given. *Both* are extremely important. One of the most pathetic things in a church is to see someone trying to exercise a spiritual gift he or she does not have. It usually ends up in utter frustration, like trying to write on a chalkboard with your toes.

DISCOVERING YOUR SPIRITUAL GIFT

In the light of the doctrine of spiritual gifts, mobilization of church members for church growth—or any other spiritual activity—must begin with whatever process is necessary for every church member to discover his or her spiritual gift. After this, the gifts must be developed and put to full use through appropriate channels and structures. But nothing can be done if believers are not able to think soberly of themselves as Romans 12:3 indicates.

How is this to be done?

It might be helpful simply to list the five steps that are necessary for discovering your spiritual gift:

1. *Explore the possibilities.* Read and study the lists of gifts in the New Testament. Know the options that appear in the Word of God so that you have something rather concrete to look for as you move ahead.

2. *Experiment with as many as possible.* If you do not try a particular gift, you will have a hard time knowing whether you have it or not. Obviously there are some gifts in the list that are hard to know how to experiment with. No one should jump off a tall building to see if they have the gift of miracles, for example. But many of them,

including the gift of evangelist, lend themselves to serious experimentation.

3. *Examine your feelings.* If you try a gift out and enjoy doing it, that is a positive indicator. On the other hand if you find yourself disliking the task the gift involves, that in itself is a fairly good sign that God hasn't given it to you.

4. *Evaluate your effectiveness.* Spiritual gifts are functional. Each one is designed to accomplish some specific objective. If you begin to think you have a certain spiritual gift be sure that you see the appropriate results when you use it. If you get no results, you may not have the gift.

5. *Expect confirmation from the Body.* No gifts can be discovered, developed, or used alone. Why? Because they are members of a total organism, the Body. If you have a spiritual gift, it will fit with others. Other Christians will recognize your gift and confirm to you that you have it. If you think you have a gift, but no one else agrees you have it, be very suspicious of your assessment in the matter.

Once these five steps are taken and surrounded with much prayer, you should be able to answer clearly and concisely when asked: "What is your spiritual gift?"

I myself have found that God has given me three: the gift of teaching, the gift of knowledge, and the missionary gift. I try to be very conscientious in using all the time and energy at my disposal in the development and use of these gifts. After all, when I come up to the final judgment, God is going to have me give an account of how I have used these gifts. I must keep in mind also that He is not going to make me account for using gifts He has never given me—and that is a comforting thought!

The Gift of Evangelist

It is obvious that the one gift above all others necessary for church growth is the gift of evangelist. This comes up in the list in Ephesians 4:11, where we are also told that the purpose of all the gifts together is the edification of the Body of Christ (see 4:12). For some reason it did not occur to me for a long time that "edification" means more than building the faith of believers, which is certainly important. It also refers to adding more cells or members to the body. In other words, it means church growth both in quantity and in quality.

Church growth occurs when the gift of evangelist is being effectively used, but it will not happen if the other gifts are not operating simultaneously. In the human body, for example, the uterus is an organ designed primarily for reproduction, but it is ineffective if the pituitary gland and the small intestine and any number of other organs are not working as they should at the same time.

It should be self-evident by now, if what we have said about spiritual gifts is valid, *not every Christian is an evangelist.* Evangelists are those Christians to whom God has given the spiritual gift of evangelist. No other members of the Body are evangelists, nor should they try to function as fingers. This is one of the main reasons why some of the efforts at "total mobilization" have ended up as frustrations and failures and have had negative rather than positive influences on church growth.

The Role of Witness

Consider now another extremely important concept: Whereas every Christian is not an *evangelist,* every Christian certainly is a *witness.* This important technical distinction prevents Christians who have spiritual gifts other than evangelist from copping out of their responsibility to share Christ with others.

In order to understand this more thoroughly, we must be clear on distinguishing between spiritual gifts and Christian roles. Gifts are the special, vocational functions that God expects each Christian to exercise on a regular basis, and different Christians will have different gifts. Roles, on the other hand, are more natural, everyday functions that all Christians are expected to exercise whenever they can.

In this sense, roles are related to fruit of the spirit as in Galatians 5:22. Love, joy, peace, and longsuffering are not gifts given to certain Christians, but fruit that God expects in the life of every Christian regardless of the gift he or she has. They are roles. As a matter of fact, the Corinthians learned that despite the fact that they had an abundance of spiritual gifts, they were ineffective because they did not combine them with the fruit of the Spirit. First Corinthians 13 was written to bring this out.

Many of the spiritual gifts have a corresponding *role*. One of the gifts, for example, is that of liberality (Rom. 12:8). Those who have that gift give their material resources to God's work in great abundance and enjoy doing it. But the corresponding role is that every Christian should give regularly to God's work (1 Cor. 16:2), and in my opinion should give something above 10 percent of his or her gross income.

Another example is the gift of faith—the kind that removes mountains (1 Cor. 12:9; 13:2). All Christians will not have this gift, but all do have a role of living a life characterized by faith, for "without faith it is impossible to please" God (Heb. 11:6).

To repeat, then, only a certain number of Christians have the *gift of evangelist,* but every Christian has the *role of witness*. These two, as we shall see, must combine to mobilize the maximum force for evangelism in your church.

The Hypothesis of the 10 Percent

If not all Christians have the gift of evangelist, how

many do? I was asking myself that question when I moved from Bolivia to the U.S.A. in 1971 because I had done enough research by then to know that the Strachan theorem was defective. I decided to take an empirical approach, so I asked the question: has any church pulled it off?

Has any church, *primarily because of the way it mobilized its membership for evangelism,* shown notable increase in church growth? The answer came quickly: The Coral Ridge Presbyterian Church in Fort Lauderdale, Florida is a bright and shining example.

So I researched the church. I read about it, I saw it on film, I visited it, and I talked to its leaders. The church was down to a low water mark of seventeen members when Pastor James Kennedy began mobilizing the membership under the program now called Evangelism Explosion. In twelve years it grew to twenty-five hundred members.

The first impression I had of the church was that everybody was in the Evangelism Explosion program, but later I found that it was not so. How many were in it? Only 250, or 10 percent of the membership. From this basis I began to develop a hypothesis which goes like this: *In the average evangelical church, up to 10 percent of the members have been given the gift of evangelist.*

For several years now I have tested this hypothesis time and time again. My graduate students, who are professional pastors and missionaries, have tested it as well. So far, it has proven to be a very realistic and workable rule of thumb, both in the U.S.A. and in Third World countries. There is, of course, somewhat of a biblical basis for this position, although the hypothesis of the 10 percent is admittedly empirical rather than evangelical.

Still, when Jesus left the earth, He left a nuclear group of about 120 committed believers in the First Church of Jerusalem. Of them, He had carefully selected and trained

10 percent—the twelve apostles—for the specific task of propagating the gospel, while the other 108 had the role of being faithful witnesses, and exercised it.

The church grew magnificently!

Some may disagree with the 10 percent figure. As time goes on, I myself have begun to suspect it may be a little high. Perhaps the range is 5 to 10 percent. But 10 percent seems both realistic and helpful.

I recall discussing the matter with Archie Parrish, when he was still heading up the Evangelism Explosion program at Coral Ridge Presbyterian Church. He reported that with a current membership of 3,000 a full 450 were active in the program. The 10 percent had become 15 percent. Wonderful!

I have a hunch, however, that this record is somewhat parallel to a baseball player's batting around .350. Years of experience have shown that anyone who can maintain a .280 or .300 average is an outstanding hitter. I think that if, year in and year out, a church can maintain 10 percent of its membership in active evangelism, it is an outstanding church. Players like Ty Cobb (.367 lifetime) and churches like Coral Ridge are unusual. In fact some years later, after he left Evangelism Explosion, Archie Parrish admitted that very thing.

As a matter of fact, if a church mobilizes the 10 percent who have the gift of evangelist, and if these people win only one convert per year—a poor showing for a person with the gift—and bring that person into church membership, the church will triple every ten years. Or, in more precise terms, the church can plan on a decadal rate of 200 percent. This is not even faith—it is a matter of simple mathematics. Faith can take the church much further.

The Problem of the Nine-Point-Five

Why then are not more churches growing at 200 percent per decade? In my opinion, one of the major obstacles to church growth today is that *of the 10 percent to whom God has given the gift of evangelist, only about one half of one percent are actively using it.* The other 9.5 percent have the gift but are not using it. Some don't know they have it, and some don't even know there is any such thing as spiritual gifts. Also, some may think they have it, but are not afforded good opportunities or proper encouragement to use it well.

A very serious problem arises when the blame is misplaced. The Strachan theorem type of "total mobilization" tends to lay blame on the 90 percent who never had the gift of evangelist in the first place. This is counterproductive since it develops unnecessary guilt complexes in the majority of church members. As a result the church can be full of gloomy and depressed Christians who (1) repel by their very attitude the new converts who are being won to Christ, yet who don't want to join a gloomy church and (2) find themselves in no psychological condition to move on and discover the spiritual gifts they do have. There is little way that a church in this condition can expect to grow.

Thus, the focus of attention for mobilizing the basic evangelistic potential of the church should be on the 9.5 percent of the members who have the gift of evangelist but are not using it. They *should* feel guilty if they are not evangelizing. If the effort is directed here, the first step toward mobilization of spiritual gifts for growth has been taken.

THE MOBILIZATION OF THE 90 PERCENT

Many churches have active and productive evangelistic programs; yet, perhaps one particular church does not grow over the years. People are being converted, baptisms are frequent, and new members are coming in all the time. But at the same time, members are drifting away.

The front door is wide open, but many who enter it soon find their way out the back door.

What is the problem here?

More often than not, the problem will lie with the 90 percent. Just because these people don't have the gift of evangelist, they should not be allowed to forget that they do have some spiritual gifts that need to be used. The nurture of the new converts and the process of folding them into the Body is equally as important as their conversion as far as church growth is concerned. Here is a crucial function of the pulpit ministry and the Sunday School.

I believe that attending adult Sunday School should be made almost a requirement for church membership. And I also believe that one of the primary objectives of the Christian education program of the church should be to enable every single person in the church, within one year after conversion in the case of adults or sometime before the twenty-fifth birthday of second-generation Christians, to come to terms with his or her spiritual gift—to know precisely what it is and to be using it effectively. If this is done, the guilt feelings that might have built up because certain people did not have certain gifts will be removed, and the whole Body will be healthy and ready for good growth.

One pastor who has done this successfully is David Libby of Trinity Congregational Church, Bolton, Massachusetts. He accepted the pastorate of a developing rural church in 1968. The church was a remodeled barn, with a sanctuary seating eighty in the front and Sunday School in the back.

After a period of ministry of healing within the Body, Libby started planning for growth. He began preaching verse-by-verse expository sermons. Some new people came in, and by the beginning of 1974 the congregation of thirty had grown to fifty.

Then all of a sudden, while preparing a sermon one day, he came up short. He was in 1 Peter, and was preparing to preach on the text: "As each one has received a gift, minister it to one another" (1 Pet. 4:10). He couldn't preach on it!

Why?

On an annual congregational survey the previous New Year, not a single member of the congregation was able to answer the question: "What is your spiritual gift?"

He changed his preaching schedule on the spot. He switched from expository to topical messages and preached twenty-two consecutive sermons on spiritual gifts! By the twenty-second Sunday both David Libby and his people were on a spiritual gift high.

He passed out a mimeographed questionnaire in the morning service in order to help people discover the gifts they never knew they had before. By the end of 1974 the congregational survey showed that every member but one had come to know what his or her spiritual gift was.

The congregation was mobilized, and ready to move!

Within four months they had to knock the wall out of the barn. On the first Sunday they went from 80 seats to 160, there was standing room only. Granted, it was Easter Sunday, but the attendance held and the church continues full. They were forced to project building a new sanctuary on their seven acres of farmland. And all this in rural New England!

As soon as I heard this, I asked David Libby how many of the twenty-five communicant members who filled out the questionnaire had the gift of evangelist. He said that two did, and he himself was not one of them. This brings up an important concept: *The pastor of a growing church does not necessarily need to have the gift of evangelist, although he or she should be very active in using the role of witness.*

The key function of the pastor, then, is not to evangelize, but to lead the people into discovering, developing and using their God-given spiritual gifts. Knowing this, the Charles E. Fuller Institute for Evangelism and Church Growth has developed a very effective *Spiritual Gifts Workshop* which any pastor or gifted lay teacher can use in a group setting. It includes the 125-question Modified Houts Questionnaire. They also distribute my book *Your Spiritual Gifts Can Help Your Church Grow.* For more information write to Box 91990, Pasadena, California 91109-1990.

Utilizing the Role of Witness

Even though it is conceded that the 90 percent who have gifts other than the gift of evangelist also have a *role of witness,* in some individuals the potential for effective use of this role for church growth is greater than in others. In order to explain this, let me set forth another hypothesis which may sound strange at first: *The effectiveness of the Christian's role as a witness for church growth decreases with that person's maturity in Christ.*

We usually assume that just the opposite is true. We feel that the longer people are Christians, the more they know about the Word of God, the deeper their prayer life, the fewer bad habits they have and, consequently, the better they are equipped for evangelism. But this is not necessarily true.

There are two good reasons for this seemingly strange phenomenon. The first is that older Christians simply have fewer contacts with non-Christians. When individuals first become Christians they start a new life, and in most cases that life centers in a new social institution called a church. If healthy Christian growth takes place, the new converts become more and more involved in the church.

Many hours of their free time are now spent with other

Christians in worship, prayer, Sunday School, committees, and church-sponsored social events. They make new friends, but almost all of them are Christians. If they are convinced believers, within two or three years all their old friends know they are Christians. They have witnessed to them, some have accepted Christ, some have decided not to become Christians and there are very few more good prospects for sharing Christ in their circle of friends and acquaintances.

Notice that the same principle applies to most second-generation Christians. Sons and daughters of Christian parents, who have been raised in the church, have fairly well limited their circle of friends to Christians, so even when they are converted their potential for evangelism is not very high compared to that of a new convert from the world.

The second reason why older Christians have very little evangelistic potential is the phenomenon called "redemption and lift." The very power of the Christian life that is generated within a new convert may soon lift him or her out of their former environment. For many, this means social and economic advance. For all, it should mean the development of a different life-style which the Bible calls "separation from the world." But as this process develops, a gap between Christians and their unsaved friends opens wider and wider, until in some cases very little can be shared with them on a deeper personal level.

This does not mean that any Christian with the role of witness may be negligent when opportunities come to lead others to Christ. All Christians at all times should be prepared for that moment when God brings them into contact with a person prepared by the Holy Spirit for accepting Christ. And they should know how to introduce that person to Christ. Here is where an ingenious device like the

Four Spiritual Laws is an invaluable tool, and the more Christians who know how to use such a tool in conjunction with their role of witness, the better.

What all this means is that *you do not build a total strategy for evangelism and church growth on this kind of occasional contact on the part of older Christians. The highest potential for evangelism through the role of witness comes from new converts who still have natural bridges to unsaved friends and relatives.* If your church runs out of new converts, its evangelistic potential drops sharply.

Putting It All Together

What is the conclusion of all that has been said? Simply this: *The greatest potential for evangelistic effectiveness in a church comes from a combination of the 10 percent of the mature Christians who have the gift of evangelist with those recent converts of less than two years in the Lord in a program planned and designed for church growth.* Put this together with the 90 percent who know and are using their other spiritual gifts, and you have developed the kind of mobilization that produces an extremely high growth potential.

STUDY QUESTIONS

1. What are some of the activities you see an enabling pastor doing?
2. Do you know what your spiritual gift or gifts are? Have you taken the steps that the author recommends?
3. How many people in your church have the gift of evangelist? Name them. What percentage of the church do they represent?

Chapter 6

HOW BIG IS BIG ENOUGH?

The third vital sign characteristic of growing churches in America is that they are big enough. By "big enough" I do not want to suggest any magic number of members for optimum size, nor do I want to give the impression that I am a superchurch addict. I thank God for some of the big churches and I thank God for some of the smaller churches. But at the same time, I am embarrassed by some of the big churches, just as I am embarrassed by some of the smaller churches.

Some time ago, for example, the *Los Angeles Times* ran a major article on the front page under the headline: "Superchurches of Radio, T.V. in Financial Bind; Naive and Sometimes Misguided Leadership by Clergymen is Blamed." Those of us in the family of God know very well that the persons mentioned by name in that article are warmhearted, dedicated servants of God who are intent on using their spiritual gifts to the maximum in winning Americans to Christ for the glory of God. They are not scoundrels or wolves in sheep's clothing, although I suppose that many non-Christians who read the *Los Angeles*

Times would have received that impression. That's what I mean by some churches being embarrassing. None of us likes our family's dirty laundry to be hung out in public.

Such publicity may also be misleading, which is even more dangerous. When some Christians hear that certain superchurches have made super mistakes they are likely to conclude that all big churches are bad. This is not a reasonable generalization.

In urban areas where 74 percent of Americans live, growing churches have become large enough to provide the variety and quality of services that members have come to expect from a modern church. This is really a fairly simple sociological principle. In our American society, with the exception of certain rural communities and among certain ethnic groups, the church is a voluntary association.

If a church meets their needs, people will become members. When it no longer meets their needs they will either drop out altogether or change churches. The more secularized a society becomes, the less inherent social pressure keeps forcing people to belong to a church, no matter what. As we all know, our American society is highly secularized and becoming more so. If churches do not match up to the people's expectations they simply cannot grow. As Robert Schuller says, "The secret of success is find a need and fill it."

BIG CHURCHES VS. SMALL CHURCHES

First of all, I want to disassociate myself from the big-church-small-church debate. The reason for this is that small churches are big enough to meet some people's needs, but other people require large churches to meet their needs.

Some people will always feel more secure in a small church. They need to sense that they are an intimate part of the whole social unit. They feel uncomfortable when they look around and see a large number of strange faces.

They also like to feel that they are needed, and thus are adverse to entering into the heavy competition for leadership that comes with a large church. They want to be missed when they are absent and they like to believe that the church wouldn't quite be the same without their membership. Obviously, a small church best meets the needs of this kind of person.

Others have a very different makeup. They need to feel that they are where the action is. They enjoy seeing piled-up traffic and long lines of Sunday School buses around their church on Sunday mornings. Posters and banners are exciting to them.

Some members of large churches appreciate the opportunity to be rather anonymous when they go to church. They don't like fusses made over them or their families. They prefer to be in a crowd where they can choose their own friends rather than having friends forced upon them. This kind of person naturally needs a large church.

Consequently, as I see it, we will have a continuing need in America for both big churches and small churches in the foreseeable future. But whether a church is large or small, *it should be a growing church.* It should be adding to its members "daily those who were being saved" (Acts 2:47). As long as there are unsaved people in its community, a church cannot be content with the status quo. Healthy large churches and healthy small churches are evangelistically effective churches.

Notice the implications of the above reasoning, however:

1. If smaller churches are growing they eventually will become large churches. Just as every river was once a stream, every large church was once a small church.

When this happens, new small churches will continually be needed.

2. Percentage-wise, the larger a church is the more people it will win to Christ, provided the same rate of conversion growth is maintained—and admittedly this is not easy to do.

Advantages of Large Churches

Generally speaking, pastors of large churches have come to feel that they can get the job of evangelism and Christian nurture done better than pastors of small churches can. All one has to do is to make the circuit of superchurch pastors' seminars and listen to the testimonies of those who hold them.

One obvious advantage they have is that—almost without exception—pastors of large churches have at one time or another also been pastors of small churches. They have seen both sides of the coin. They have a personal point of comparison.

The opposite, however, is rarely true—very few pastors of small churches have ever been pastors of large churches. I suppose this helps explain why church growth people generally listen well when pastors of large churches tell how they do it.

Up to a point, I can empathize with the impatience that pastors of large churches have with much of the criticism that is leveled against them. I am not a pastor, but my own Lake Avenue Congregational Church has thirty-five hundred members and falls into the large church category. When I mention this, I often get the response: "Oh, that's too big!"

But I have learned to reply: "Too big for what?" The answer to that one is hard to come by.

Our church is not too big to provide a first-rate pulpit ministry. It's not too big to put together a professionally executed worship service that brings believers into soul-stirring contact with God every Sunday morning. It's not too big to provide a vital youth program geared to the special needs of each age group. It's not too big to provide expert pastoral counseling.

It's not too big to offer opportunities for close friendships, more casual acquaintances, vital community involvement, sound biblical teaching, openings for Christian service of all kinds, a missionary program that makes a difference in world evangelization, the finest in sacred music, and . . . I could go on and on.

The major reason a large church can provide these services is that it can afford to hire a well-trained and experienced staff. Running a modern church in America is a professional job. The very existence of theological seminaries verifies this fact. They are designed as clearly for professional training as medical schools are in their field.

Notice also that larger churches not only can hire more people who are specialists in one field or another, but they can also afford to pay them enough to keep them. It may not seem spiritual, but there is a discernible relationship between salary scales and ministerial longevity. And, it is a fact that churches which keep pastors longer are more likely to grow. Pastors are people too, and if they are comfortable they are less likely to be looking around for greener pastures.

Except for providing a comfortable environment for those people who feel insecure with excitement and strangers, a large church can do just about everything a small church can do, but not vice versa. A church can be *too small* for lots of things. I think, for example, that our church, at thirty-five hundred members, may be too small for a highly effective singles ministry. I began to suspect this when I heard Robert Schuller say that their singles program limped along until their church passed the five thousand membership mark. When they were over five thousand total members they had enough single adults in each age bracket to grade the program properly—and then it soared. Jim Smoke's expert opinion is that a critical mass of 350 single adults is needed for a dynamic urban singles ministry today.

Speaking of Robert Schuller, consider how he presents the big church vs. small church matter to potential converts. His church subscribes to the Telecredit service which gives him a printout of all the closings on residential property purchases in his area. His staff sends out twenty-seven thousand form letters per year to new families in the neighborhood.

On the very first page of the form letter, a sub-title appears: "The Smallest Church and the Biggest Church in Orange County." In it he says, "While over 7,000 people attend the five services every Sunday, we have it structured in such a way that people who like small churches can attend the little Chapel-in-the-Sky at the top of the Tower where they have a view from the Santa Ana mountains to Catalina Island floating in the ocean beyond the coast line."

Everyone knows, of course, that this is a come-on. It is designed to get them to go to the "small church" and in the process try the "big church" as well. It's the "try it, you'll like it" approach.

The fact of the matter is that if only 3 percent of the members of the Crystal Cathedral attended the Chapel-in-the-Sky, there would be standing room only every Sunday. It seats only two hundred. But many who try it like it, as the Crystal Cathedral's sustained growth rate of 500 percent per decade has indicated.

Bigness as an Evangelistic Tool

The attraction of a complete church program designed

to meet all kinds of human needs can be a powerful evangelistic tool. Few know how to exploit this potential as well as does Robert Schuller. He does it big once a year—on Easter Sunday. On the theory that more unchurched people are willing to listen to the claims of Christ on Easter than any other day of the year, the Crystal Cathedral pulls out all the stops on that day.

I recall one Easter Sunday bulletin which was much more than a bulletin; it was a sixteen-page, tabloid-sized advertising extravaganza. What did it advertise? All the services that the Crystal Cathedral offers to meet a wide variety of needs of the people in Orange County. It reproduced articles on the church from *Time, Christian Life,* and *Los Angeles Times* to let people know that they have come to a place where some notable action is occurring.

The bulletin tells them about personalized pastoral counseling so people will not think church members are just a computer number. It advertises Sunday School and Bible teaching programs for children, young people, and adults. It offers the various singles programs. And it tells them of opportunities for backpacking, camping, sports, boating, and other activities for youth.

The bulletin goes on to describe musical programs in no less than sixteen choirs. It invites women to candlelight dinners and a luncheon with Mrs. Jack LaLanne. It lets them know about the "Hour of Power" television ministry nationwide. And the center spread splashes out the architect's drawing of their planned facility expansion.

One of the objectives of this massive promotional effort is to get the unchurched Easter visitor back the following Sunday. For many years Schuller delivered "The Greatest Sermon Ever Preached," a completely choreographed recitation of Jesus' Sermon on the Mount, and which has to qualify as one of the most spectacular pulpit presentations in contemporary Christendom. From there the inquirers are enrolled in the pastor's class where they are led to a personal relationship with Jesus Christ and then into church membership.

How About the Smaller Churches?

I realize that it is not easy for everyone to identify with a superchurch like the Crystal Cathedral. Even when we remember that there was a time not too long ago when it had 50 members, 100 members, 350 members and so forth, not many churches in America are where it is now.

According to Lyle Schaller's research, a full 95 percent of the churches in America average under 350 for Sunday morning worship. Half the churches in the country have 75 or less out on Sunday morning. This means that if you have 100 out on Sunday morning you are well above average, and if you have 400, you are a very big church by comparative standards.

But the chances are that your church, whatever the membership, is not big enough. The chances are that you would do well to put church growth principles into practice and trust God for a 100 percent or 200 percent increase over the next ten years. I do not believe that every church must grow or can grow. But I do believe that a large number of plateaued and declining churches should wake up and receive the growth that God intends them to have.

Willys Braun did an enlightening piece of research in connection with a church growth project in the Christian and Missionary Alliance, a denomination of relatively small churches. It shows that even among small churches, the slightly larger ones seem to be more suited for effective evangelism than the slightly smaller ones.

During "Operation Harvest" in 1972, it was found that C&MA churches which had membership ranging from 150-200 members produced the greatest percentage of converts. Churches that size are the biggies in the Alliance, with only 4 percent of Alliance churches that large. But those 4 percent of the churches produced a full 31 percent of the total denominational growth!

Braun's observation was stated graphically: "We could have had the same growth if by some sort of National League trade arrangement we had exchanged 1,147 of our other churches for 193 more of this size!"

More directly, Braun questioned the value of budgeting denominational funds for churches in the 1–125 membership category, when the investment of the same funds in the churches of the 125–150 category, to help them move to the 150–200 level, would undoubtedly result in accelerated church growth for the denomination as a whole. For the Alliance, evidently, 125 members in a church is not quite big enough.

Braun didn't raise the question, but I wonder how a half dozen Alliance churches of 500–600 members might compare to the rest? Possibly the top 4 percent would do even better if they were larger.

THE OPTIMUM GROWTH FACTOR

This brings us to the next question: How big is big enough? Suppose you do move into a pattern of growth—is there any optimum growth level you should aim for?

The optimum growth factor is not a frequent topic of discussion in the writings of pastors or superchurches. One does not find Jerry Falwell or W.A. Criswell or James Kennedy setting limits on their growth. This is understandable since exercising leadership in large, growing churches is part and parcel of the very life-style of these pastors.

Robert Schuller says: "One thing is certain: a church must never stop growing. When it ceases to grow it will start to die."

But I feel there may be a danger here. Postulating

unlimited expansion growth may turn out to be deceptive and ultimately counterproductive. There must be a limit to the growth of a local congregation somewhere.

To put it into perspective, however, the largest church in the world is the Yoido Full Gospel Church of Seoul, Korea with 350 thousand members at this writing and a projected membership of one half million before the end of 1984. Pastor Paul Yonggi Cho preaches to well over 100 thousand persons each Sunday in seven services. He is expanding his 10 thousand-seat sanctuary to accommodate between 25 thousand and 35 thousand. And the Young Nak Presbyterian Church, also of Seoul, is constructing what will be another of the world's largest sanctuaries seating 20 thousand. Their membership is currently 60 thousand. Pastor Javier Vasquez of the Jotabeche Methodist Pentecostal Church in Santiago, Chile, allows his 80 thousand members to come to the main sanctuary only one Sunday night per month because it seats only 16 thousand persons. The other Sundays they are ministering in forty satellite churches around the city, some of which are two thousand and three thousand in size.

Will we ever have churches this size in America? Possibly. The largest is Jack Hyles' First Baptist of Hammond, Indiana, with a total membership of 74,500 and weekly attendance of 18,500. Highland Park Baptist of Chattanooga, Tennessee counts 57,000 members and First Baptist of Dallas over 22,000. I am aware of four churches in the U.S. which in the near future will have sanctuaries seating 10,000. As churches like these grow, we learn more and more about optimum growth factors.

By raising the issue of optimum growth, therefore, I do not want to be forced to set certain numbers as a limit. David Mains discusses limits in his book *Full Circle* and sets 200 as the optimum level for Circle Church, Chicago. And in *Christianity Today,* James Davey argues that an ideal optimum size for a church in America is one of 400–600 members. But some of the superchurches see it differently.

The Philosophy of Ministry

Rather than dealing with specific figures myself, however, I would like to attempt to articulate some principles. And the first one is this: *The optimum size of each church depends primarily on its philosophy of ministry.*

Churches, much like people, have distinct personalities that set them apart one from another. Some of their personalities happen to be rather undesirable, and thus they do not attract many new members.

But others, particularly the growing churches, have developed fascinating personalities. They have characteristics that to one degree or another give the church a self-identity that makes it unique.

Park Street Church of Boston, Grace Community Church of the Valley (Panorama City, California), Calvary Temple of Denver, and Bel Air Presbyterian of Los Angeles, for example, are all magnificent churches—but vastly different from one another. Underlying each church personality is a distinct philosophy of ministry.

Just as every Christian has a spiritual gift, every church has a philosophy of ministry. Some know what it is and can articulate it; some don't realize there is any such thing.

Unlike spiritual gifts, however, some philosophies of ministry are good and some are not so good. But the first thing a church needs to know before it can come to terms with its optimum growth factor is its philosophy of ministry.

The philosophy of ministry of Lake Avenue Congregational Church, for example, is based on three specific priorities and seven expectations. Circle Church's philosophy of ministry is described by them as the "open church" concept which is heavy on mixing people of different ethnic backgrounds. Peninsula Bible Church in Palo Alto, California calls their philosophy of ministry "body life." The Church of the Redeemer in Houston has built a philosophy of ministry around the concept of charismatic Christian community.

There are many good philosophies of ministry and each one will tend to determine certain levels of optimum growth.

Minimum Optimum Growth

What is the guiding principle for determining a level of *minimum optimum growth*? Simply this—a church is not large enough if it cannot yet meet two requirements: (1) It must be large enough for the efficient functioning of its own philosophy of ministry; (2) it must be large enough to provide an adequate base for extension growth.

Part of the technical terminology of church growth is the fourfold classification of *internal growth, expansion growth, extension growth* and *bridging growth:*

Internal growth includes all that happens within the Body of Christ among believers. Worship, Christian nurture, counseling, revival, or anything that makes Christians better servants of God is internal growth.

Expansion Growth occurs when believers move out into the world, win people to Christ and bring them into church membership in their own local congregation. It results in membership growth of the local assembly.

Extension growth means winning people to Christ, but instead of bringing them into the same local church, they are gathered into new churches. It is also called church planting, and new congregations result.

Bridging growth also means planting new churches, but in cultures different from the culture of the base church. The cross-cultural aspect makes it a more complex process than extension growth.

In these terms, then, there is obviously no optimum growth limit on extension and bridging growth as long as there are people in the world who have yet to become Christians. With 2.7 billion people in Asia, Africa and Latin America who have not yet heard of Jesus Christ, and with over 100 million unchurched people right here in the United States, there is no way a concerned Christian can talk about optimum *extension* or *bridging* growth.

The Need for Extension Growth

As a matter of fact, I do not hear nearly enough talk about extension growth here in our country. Very few of the churches cited so far have incorporated as a specific part of their regular planning and budget a program to plant new churches.

I have been somewhat disappointed to find such a low level of concern for church planting on the part of American pastors, but at the same time encouraged to see a clear upsurge of interest at the beginning of the decade of the eighties. Several seminaries are now teaching practical courses in church planting. I myself teach one at Fuller Seminary.

It is only natural that when a church does begin to reproduce offspring that these offspring develop a philosophy of ministry similar to that of the mother church. Thus, the number of people necessary for minimum optimum growth will vary according to the philosophy of ministry of the mother church.

Circle Church is realistic in setting a figure of two hundred as their minimum optimum growth level. One church in Phoenix, Arizona has set an ideal of six hundred members and has spun off several new congregations in order to stay around that level. Another church might say they need twelve hundred members.

An excellent model for a practical application of the optimum growth principle is Redwood Chapel of Castro Valley, California. Pastor Sherman Williams' philosophy of ministry involves a strong emphasis on the development of small, professional-quality musical groups and a television ministry. Integral to their church program also is the planting of a new church with their philosophy of ministry every two years. Their minimum optimum level is around nine hundred.

Maximum Optimum Growth

Facilities always have a good deal to do with determining the *maximum optimum growth level.* A growing church which has arrived at its minimum optimum level will eventually need to face the decision of whether to expand facilities, and if so, how much. In most cases, what your church hopes to accomplish on Sunday morning will provide a reasonable criterion for future planning. And this again comes back to the church's philosophy of ministry.

Robert Schuller's main objective on Sunday morning is to impress unchurched people in Orange County. He lives in an area of super shopping centers, Disneyland, Knott's Berry Farm, Anaheim Stadium, and the Anaheim Convention Center. Unchurched people there are oriented to the big, the spectacular and the exciting.

Dr. Schuller outgrew his seventeen-hundred-seat sanctuary and fifteen-hundred-automobile drive-in parking lot a number of years ago. He was faithful to his philosophy of ministry when he projected a three-thousand-seat Crystal Cathedral, clearly designed to impress the unchurched. The $20 million structure itself set a limit of growth for the congregation, however, and membership peaked at twelve thousand. The church plateaued a number of years ago, but has been instrumental in planting some new churches in both California and Florida.

A similar program would not fit the philosophy of ministry of Lake Avenue Congregational Church. Pastor Paul Cedar's objective on Sunday morning is not so much to impress the unchurched as it is to develop a worship experience that brings Christians into the very presence of God. He and his associate, Dan Bird, have established a whole theology of worship which by general consensus is one of the primary factors contributing to the growth of that church. This kind of worship can best be accomplished in a sanctuary of around twenty-five hundred. So the maximum optimum growth for Lake Avenue Church might be somewhat less than for the Crystal Cathedral.

But there is nothing magic about these numbers. A smaller maximum around 350 is realistic for Circle Church and 900 is considered both minimum and maximum for Redwood Chapel. Since their sanctuary doubles as a television studio, Redwood Chapel's seating capacity of 650 is considered ideal, and Pastor Williams intends to keep to two Sunday morning worship services. Surplus people are used to plant new churches.

In summary, *a growing church can consider itself big enough when it is effectively winning lost people to Christ, when it provides the range of services that meet the needs of its members, and when it is reproducing itself by planting new churches.*

STUDY QUESTIONS

1. What are some of the advantages of a large church? How does your church relate in size? Do you feel the emphasis quoted by the author of Robert Schuller's Crystal Cathedral on Easter is a practical one for you?

2. What do you think about the author's recommendation as to optimum size of a church? What is your church growth philosophy? Has it been clearly stated? Are you following a specific plan towards a set goal membership and/or average attendance?

3. Has your church ever had a "daughter" church? Are you even pregnant with one? Do you have any intention of ever having offspring?

Chapter 7

CELEBRATION + CONGREGATION + CELL = CHURCH

The fourth vital sign of a healthy, growing church can be best expressed by this simple formula: Celebration + Congregation + Cell = Church

What does this mathematical expression mean. Let's take it apart and consider it one element at a time, beginning with the first: celebration.

CELEBRATION

One of the things a large church can do well is to celebrate. By "celebrate," I mean roughly what most people mean by "worship," but not entirely. A person can worship God beside a babbling brook in a forest or in his car on a freeway or with his family around the dinner table.

However, none of these situations is conducive to what I mean by celebration. The occasion for that in most churches is on Sunday morning. When a lot of people come together, hungry to meet God, a *special* kind of worship experience can occur. That experience is what I want to call "celebration."

While the relationship is not a direct proportion, size has something to do with the quality of a celebration. As every sports fan knows there is something about a game played before seventy-five thousand spectators that makes it superior to the same game before fifteen hundred. As every sociologist knows, certain laws of collective behavior operate differently in small groups than in large groups. As every psychologist knows, mob psychology has certain effects on people's emotions and their reactions to stimuli which would not be the case at all if the person were alone or in a small group.

Worship as a Festival

God's people have known about celebration for a long time. The fact that the Temple was the focal point for the worship of Jehovah helped immensely in keeping the twelve tribes of Israel and their respective clans together as the people of God. The Temple was so designed that lots of people would be there at one time seeking God and seeing others do the same thing.

By divine appointment not only was there a weekly Sabbath, but great yearly festivals such as the Passover, Pentecost, Day of Atonement, the Feast of Tabernacles, and later Purim and others. Something good happened to God's people during those celebrations that would not have happened without them.

Christian festivals and celebrations have been a longstanding tradition in American Christianity, too, although they have taken on different forms and names at different times. The great camp meetings of a century ago, Finney's revivals, Billy Graham's crusades, summer Bible conferences, Urbana missionary conventions—all these have operated basically as celebrations. They were and still are functional substitutes for the Jewish festivals. Christians love to go to them. They are a lot of fun!

Some Sunday morning worship services in our churches are fun, too. Unfortunately, however, the Sunday morning service in many churches is more like a funeral than a festival. There is nothing unauthentic about that kind of worship service—true, committed Christians can and do get through to God under such circumstances. But it is not the kind of experiences that they are very enthusiastic in inviting their unconverted friends to. Why not admit it? It's no fun!

This is probably one reason why many churches have remained small over the years. Most of them, especially when a new pastor has arrived, have tried to beef up their worship service from time to time so it would be attractive to outsiders. But, with some notable exceptions, nothing seems to work. The problem could very well be that the churches are simply too small. Good celebrations need lots of people to make them fun and attractive.

For several years my pastor was Raymond C. Ortlund. Under his ministry I learned a great deal about worship. For Ortlund, "Worship is top priority. Everything, absolutely everything, must be put aside to do this thing that God has called you to do. Worship is lofty business—but, friend, we do it so poorly."

Ortlund knew that good worship does not just happen. It has to be planned and worked on. Through the years he set such a standard of excellence in worship that when a pastoral change was made, one of the chief qualifications for his successor was the ability to maintain the standard. Paul Cedar has done remarkably, and under his leadership the worship at Lake Avenue Congregational Church has remained a key point of attraction for members and nonmembers alike.

Both Ortlund and Cedar have spared no effort or expense in recruiting the best of professional help for the worship life of the church. Ortlund teamed up with Bruce Leafblad, now a professor at Southwestern Baptist Theological Seminary. Cedar has Dan Bird who possesses what many churches need: a spiritual gift for designing recipes that combine choirs and Scripture and preaching and announcements and organ music and offerings and prayer and solos and standing and sitting and noise and silence in such a way that fifty-two times a year three thousand people go home to Sunday dinner feeling that they have just had an important meeting with almighty God and that because of it they are not the same.

"Playing Church"

Worship, of course, can never be a one-way street. With all the skill in the world on the platform and in the pulpit, a person in the pew will not meet God if he or she doesn't put anything into it. Christian people have to be motivated and trained to worship well or they will end up "playing church." In our church we are told from the pulpit to avoid playing church with the same finality that we are told to avoid cheating, stealing or adultery. Anne Ortlund's book, *Up with Worship,* says it as well as anyone has.

This is not at all to say that Lake Avenue Congregational Church has the best or the *only* kind of celebration that will help a church to grow. We do know that it is good for our people in our community at this particular point of history, and we wouldn't trade it for anything. Yet I have seen dozens of other equally effective patterns of celebration so different from my own church's that a person from Mars might wonder if it was the same religion. But if these celebrations bring people to God in such a way that they say to their unchurched friends, "Hey, how about coming to church with me—you'll have a great time!" they will help the church grow.

CONGREGATION

I know when I find a growing church, I will also find a well-executed celebration. However, a good celebration alone does not make for a healthy, growing church. The celebration will generally be there, but it will also be properly balanced with the other two major functions of a local church: congregation and cell.

Celebration + Congregation + Cell = Church. Many growing churches combine all three of these elements.

The distinction between the celebration and the congregation is a crucial one. Some avoid a large celebration because they feel that if they encourage too many people to gather together on a Sunday morning they will lose the sense of personal fellowship, which they value very highly. They are concerned that a Christian in a large celebration might be anonymous. They even feel that fellowship and worship must be so closely related that they plan church seating in a circle rather than in rows. They want eye contact with each other rather than with those on the platform.

Eye contact and fellowship are necessary, but in the congregation and cell, *not* in the celebration. Anonymity in a celebration is not bad at all. The fact that I am not acquainted with the persons in front of me or behind me in Dodger Stadium, for example, has no effect on my personal involvement in the game.

The same thing applies when I go to church to worship God on Sunday morning. I don't go there to widen my circle of friends or discuss and dialogue. My goal is to meet God, and that ultimately involves just God and me. Anne Ortlund believes so strongly in this that she titled one of the chapters of *Up with Worship,* "Three Cheers for Stiff, Rigid Rows of Pews!" Well said!

However, if all a church has to offer is celebration, it may well not be a balanced church. Kathryn Kuhlman's monthly Sunday afternoon meetings in Los Angeles' Shrine Auditorium were great celebrations. Billy Graham rallies are great celebrations. Bill Gothard seminars produce another kind of celebration. But none of these in itself is a church, precisely because the participants—by the nature of the gatherings—maintain anonymity.

In the congregation the anonymity is lost. If believers miss two or three celebrations in a row, no one is the wiser. But if they miss two or three meetings of the "congregation," they are worried over, called upon, prayed for, and made to understand that there are people around who care. Deep down, everyone needs to have others know his or her name and use it. The congregation is the place where people know each other's names.

Congregation as a Fellowship Circle

I think I first latched on to the term *congregation* when I read Larry Richards' book, *A New Face for the Church.* He uses *congregation* in relationship to the word *cell,* and I like the terminology. Lyle Schaller, who is more sociologically oriented, calls it a *fellowship circle,* in contrast to the whole church which he calls the *membership circle.* I like this terminology also, although Schaller's *fellowship circle* includes both of what I join Larry Richards in calling the congregation *and* the cell. In some denominational settings, such as Lutheran, the whole church is commonly referred to as the congregation, so it might be better there to call these fellowship groups *sub-congregations.*

The major characteristic of the congregation, as I see it, is that everyone in the congregation is supposed to know everyone else. Here is where fellowship starts, although it does not end here. In smaller churches, of course, the fellowship group and the membership group are likely to be one and the same. In a church of up to a hundred or two hundred members you are supposed to identify a stranger who wanders in on Sunday morning, and you expect to be missed if for some reason you don't attend.

But not so in a larger church. The congregations there take forms other than that of the membership group. Undoubtedly the most common form of a congregation within a larger church is the adult Sunday School class. But it can take other forms as well. It can be structured as a neighborhood group which meets regularly. It can be a charismatic prayer meeting. It can be a task-oriented group such as the choir or the evangelism team, or the bus ministry leaders, or the commission on social involvement. It can be activity-oriented such as a softball team or a camping club. In many ways—except for formal worship, these several congregations within the larger church function exactly like a small country church would be expected to function.

Churches can grow for a time with just a great celebration. But such growth can be illusory. This is one reason for using composite membership figures whenever possible. They balance off Sunday morning attendance and church membership rolls against involvement in congregations, most readily measured by Sunday School attendance.

New York vs. Dallas

Pastor Harold Fickett rigorously applied the principle of balancing the celebration with the congregation as he led the Van Nuys, California First Baptist Church from a membership of thirty-seven hundred to twelve thousand in his pastorate of sixteen years—a decadal rate of 109 percent. He learned it from comparing the histories of First Baptist, New York City with First Baptist, Dallas.

The First Baptist Church of New York was one of the great Christian centers of the nation around the turn of the century. Pastor I.M. Haldemann was an outstanding man of God and such an exciting preacher that people would line up for blocks just to get a seat at one of his services.

The celebration was superb, the church grew, and it is still fondly remembered as a powerful lighthouse for the gospel. But when Haldemann left, decline set in, and now First Baptist is only a shadow of what it once was.

At around the same time, Pastor George Truett was developing a similarly influential church at First Baptist, Dallas. He matched Haldemann's pulpit ability and served his church for forty years. Many people thought that when Truett left, the church would decline. But it did not. The church continued strong when he left thirty years ago, and it has become even stronger under the following pastor, W.A. Criswell.

As Harold Fickett explains it in his book, *Hope for Your Church,* the major difference between the two churches was the strong Christian education program developed in Dallas. By the time Truett left, his staff had built the largest Sunday School in the South. In other words, both churches had a wonderful celebration, but the one that ultimately survived combined *celebration* with *congregation.*

Decentralizing Big Churches

While it is true that almost every growing church has developed congregations or fellowship groups within the total church, I feel that in many cases they can be strengthened even more by a careful process of decentralization. If properly decentralized, they can contribute to church growth in a much more powerful way. This decentralization takes two forms: (1) multiplication of congregations and (2) a higher degree of self-government.

Some years ago a fascinating experiment was run by Richard Myers, a sociologist of religion from Indiana. He reports in *Program Expansion: The Key to Church Growth* how he divided a number of ministers into two groups. The first group agreed that whenever a Sunday School teacher resigned, they would combine that class with another similar class. The second group agreed that in every department a new teacher would be added and given a new class formed from the existing classes in the department. In other words, the first group reduced the total number of classes and the second group increased the total number of classes. At the end of a year they were to report the results.

What happened?

In the first group, every combined class had decreased in size until it was no larger than either of the two classes that had joined together. In the second group, every class had grown to the size of the other classes before dividing.

This helps confirm what I have long suspected: *If a church makes the multiplication of congregations or fellowship groups a definite part of its planning for growth, the church will increase its growth potential.*

How Large Is a Congregation?

What is the optimum size for a congregation? This needs to be discussed lest some groupings be considered congregations which aren't congregations at all. The largest Sunday School class I ever attended was Jack Hyles' Pastor's Class which preceded the morning worship service in First Baptist, Hammond, Indiana. I suppose there were around fifteen hundred adults in this class which met in the sanctuary. This group is clearly too big to be considered a congregation or a fellowship group. First Baptist does have congregations, of course, but this should not be counted as one of them.

Just as in the case of the optimum growth of the church as a whole, the *minimum optimum growth* of a congregation will first be determined by its secondary purpose—the primary being fellowship. A softball team of twenty-five is plenty big enough. But twenty-five might be too small for a fellowship group of single adults.

The *maximum optimum growth* of a congregation is limited by its primary objective of fellowship. In the first edition of this book, I suggested that 250 might be a maximum for a meaningful fellowship group. The research I have done since then has brought the figure considerably lower. I now think the ideal size of the congregation will run between 30 and 80. With some special dynamics, particularly a strong release of ministry through spiritual gifts, a congregation can exceed 80 and grow to 100 or 120. But ordinarily when it gets to be that size or larger the experience of fellowship is considerably reduced.

Managing the continuous organization of new congregations as the church grows should be of central concern to a church growth pastor. Very rarely will the initiative to start a new group arise within the existing congregations. The direction must come from the pastor or a designated staff member if the system is going to operate smoothly. Failure to do this is a frequent cause of stagnation both in small churches which desire to move past the 200 barrier and in large churches as well. The only exception I have found is in some churches of the very wealthy who buy into fellowship groups such as country clubs or yacht clubs and who do not need their church to meet their needs for fellowship.

Self-Government Is Needed

Multiplication of congregation or fellowship groups is the first aspect of decentralization. The second involves a degree of self-government in the congregations themselves.

The suggestion of congregational self-government may be a hard one for churches with an Episcopal or Presbyterian form of government to accept. And it may be rather difficult also for many churches with congregational forms of government to accept. Nevertheless, latent energy for growth within a church will be released if each congregation of adults in the church gains a measure of self-determination.

I came to this realization myself when studying the growth figures of my former congregation, the Mariners Class in Lake Avenue Congregational Church. While our church as a whole is growing and our Sunday School is growing, our class of young grandparents' age had declined 43 percent over five years. The class had about 125 active members.

The Bible teaching was first rate. The class members were warm and friendly and happy. The spiritual tone was high. The physical setting was ideal. But something was wrong or we wouldn't have been declining at such a rate.

While our size could have been a problem, it seemed like something else was wrong. My hunch was that some aspect of our church *structure* was at fault. The first clue of this came when I began to inquire about who was directly responsible for the growth or decline of the Mariners Class. Since it was decline in this case rather than growth, I found the answer rather elusive.

Some said the pastoral staff had the responsibility, some said the Christian education committee and some said the executive committee of the Mariners Class. Significantly, no one suggested that it might be the class itself. Why? Because at that time (and it is no longer the case) the class was so structured that the membership was responsible for no major decision involving its own activities. All major decisions affecting the class were passed down from somewhere above.

When I realized this, I had to ask: What happened to old-fashioned congregationalism? Congregational churches like ours were founded in colonial New England on the principle that every adult member ought to have an active voice in his or her church affairs. This principle works well as long as the church has not passed the maximum size for a true congregation.

But when it gets to thirty-five hundred like ours, the church has long since ceased being a congregation. This is undoubtedly one of the reasons why we have had difficulty in gathering a quorum for church business meetings. Everyone knows that it is impossible for a huge business meeting to make really crucial decisions, so they stay home when one is called.

The question then becomes: How can large congregational churches maintain the strengths of congregationalism? The answer is both obvious and significant: *Multiply adult congregations within the church and let each enjoy its own congregational form of government.*

In a smaller congregation, the members feel that they have a significant piece of the ownership. The creativity of the members should be allowed to surface, and each congregation decide on its structure, leadership, and philosophy of ministry. Many programs of ministry and outreach can be originated in the congregations. Spiritual gifts can be discovered and used in the setting of a congregation to a much greater degree than in the larger church.

I have found this to be true in a relatively new adult class which I helped organize and now teach, called the "120 Fellowship." It is a class with a high level of awareness of spiritual gifts. What I consider to be an extraordinary degree of mutual love, support, and caring has developed in the class. Several have the spiritual gift of pastor, both men and women. My objective is to see ministry within the class developed to such an intensity that no member of the class will have to approach those on the professional pastoral staff of the church for one-on-one ministry.

At the same time, we take pains not to become a

church within a church. The pastoral staff is informed of and approves the class's philosophy of ministry. The money that the class raises for its own projects is giving over and above the tithes and offerings promised for the church's overall budget. In the Sunday morning sessions the class holds no worship service and does no congregational singing. The focus of worship is the celebration of the whole church, and the class has no inclination to compete in this area of ministry. Members of the class are taught to be loyal to Lake Avenue Congregational Church and to its staff.

I feel so strongly about the need for combining the membership group with the fellowship group that I think joining a congregation ought to be a *membership requirement* for an adult joining a church. As a part of the membership class, the adult candidates should be required to become aware of the various congregations, visit the appropriate ones and, by the time they are taken into membership, decide which congregation they want to join. If this were done it would strengthen a church as steel rods strengthen poured concrete.

THE CELL

The third part of the formula is the cell. I mentioned before that the congregation is only the beginning of the fellowship circle. It is possible to fellowship with eighty other people, but it is not possible to enter into the deeper kind of interpersonal relationships that are necessary to meet another important set of human needs. The cell, sometimes called a *small group,* is a very special relationship. It is so close to a family situation that I like to call it a *kinship circle* to contrast it from the membership circle and the fellowship circle.

I would feel less than honest at this point if I failed to admit that I am not by nature a small group person, nor is my wife. However, I do listen to my pastor who has told me more than once: "You're a fine Christian, but you'll be a much better one if you let God get a hold of you in a small group." I think he's probably right, and I keep trying, but feebly.

I also listen to people like Larry Richards who have a deep personal involvement in spreading the small group movement through churches in America. Here is how he defines the cell: "Eight or twelve believers gathered to minister to each other, to grow in their sensed love and unity, and to encourage one another to full commitment to Christ."

While small cell groups have proved to be a significant dynamic for growth in most churches, research has indicated that they are not for everyone. Some people in rural areas where their extended family lives in close proximity, for example, are not usually inclined toward participation in small church groups. There is little need for such groups in communities where church members see each other frequently outside of church activities. Some with a low level of verbal skills feel very uncomfortable in a cell group where spiritual intimacy and accountability is developed. Exceptions should be made for such people, and they should not be allowed to develop guilt complexes if they are not socially or psychologically adaptable to small groups.

Daniel Baumann, former pastor of the Whittier Area Baptist Fellowship, has utilized the small group dynamic for church growth as well as anyone else I am aware of. His church, a spinoff from another Baptist church, began with 350 members in 1971 and grew steadily to 820 members in four years. This figures out to a rate of 740 percent per decade, and this in spite of a facilities problem caused by their sharing a church building with a church of another denomination.

Baumann feels that one of the keys to their growth was what he calls their "Circles of Concern" program. The purpose of this program is "to help us reach out to the other members of the Body of Christ, to assure that no person who comes to our church ever leaves feeling alone or unwanted, but is involved in a meaningful relationship with others who show love and personal concern."

Each Circle of Concern starts with approximately four couples. Children are also included. The average size is six family units in each circle. They are required to meet at least once a month and also to become involved in some kind of service to the community.

Many meet frequently as well for meals together or for other social events such as a camping trip or a ball game. At the end of each year the circles normally disband and are reorganized with new people. Exceptions to this are allowed if for some reason a particular circle wishes to continue as is.

In 1975 the church counted 32 active Circles of Concern. This means that 192 *families* had developed a level of activity and commitment far above that of the average church member in America. It contributed to a dynamic growth situation in the Whittier Area Baptist Fellowship, and a similar kind of program will contribute to church growth just about wherever it is put into practice.

Remember: *Celebration + Congregation + Cell = Church.*

FREE METHODIST CHURCH
4th & Sycamore Streets
VINCENNES, INDIANA

STUDY QUESTIONS

1. Is your church celebration worship service a festival or a funeral? What could be done to stimulate more life in the service?

2. Do you know everyone in your congregation? Do you *belong to* a congregation? Do you have a number of congregations in your church?
3. What kind of activities characterize a cell? Are you a member of a cell? If so describe the activity to the rest of the group.

Chapter 8

TO EACH HIS OWN! WHY?

The fifth vital sign of a healthy, growing church is that its membership is composed of basically one kind of people.

Even in church, "birds of a feather flock together." And in church growth terminology this is called the "homogeneous unit principle." Its classic expression is found in Donald McGavran's *Understanding Church Growth:* "People like to become Christians without crossing racial, linguistic or class barriers."

A "homogeneous unit" is simply a group of people who consider each other to be "our kind of people." They have many areas of mutual interest. They share the same culture. They socialize freely. When they are together they are comfortable and they all feel at home.

Of all the scientific hypotheses developed within the church growth framework, this is one of the most consistently observed worldwide. Two decades of research dealing with numerous cultures in virtually every corner of the world confirms that the churches most likely to grow are those which bring together in the local fellowship those of a single homogeneous unit.

THE HOMOGENEOUS UNIT DEBATE

I have spent much time discussing and debating the homogeneous unit principle with Christian leaders of many countries of the world. Without doubt, it is the most controversial of all church growth principles. *Eternity* magazine, for example, published a feature article under the title "Where Church Growth Fails the Gospel" which attacked the homogeneous unit principle with a great deal of verve. My book on the subject, *Our Kind of People* (John Knox), provoked a review article, written with intense irritation, entitled, "Evangelism Without the Gospel."

Why the controversy?

Unfortunately, many Americans find the homogeneous unit principle very difficult to accept. Americans, particularly those with a college education, seem to have a strong, inherent resistance to approving churches of just one kind of people. Yet missionaries and Christian leaders from other countries generally accept it almost as a matter of course.

In Burundi, for example, Christian Tutsis have little problem in understanding why Hutus prefer their own kind of local church with their own leadership. Bolivian mestizos tend to give liberty to Bolivian Aymaras to form their kind of church. In Singapore, Malaysian churches and Indian churches and Chinese churches are mutually accepted alongside each other. French Christians do not seem to have difficulty with Gypsies gathering together in Gypsy churches.

In America, homogeneous unit churches are also the rule. It is simply a sociological fact of life. Even an uninitiated foreigner could readily see that in one city there are Hispanic churches, Oriental churches, Anglo churches, European churches, and black churches. A more skillful observer might be able to detect differences between

Cuban and Mexican, Japanese and Korean, blue collar and executive, Romanian and Polish, American black and West Indian black. And even more subtle subdivisions eventually become very important as factors for church growth.

But, while most Americans will admit that homogeneous churches do exist, many will not go on to say that they *ought* to exist. In other words it poses an ethical problem for them which grew very acute during the civil rights upheavals of the 1960s when the black-white racial struggles seemed to be tearing apart the very fabric of our society.

At a time when racial sensitivities were worn thin, Christian intellectuals developed theologies that led to the conclusion that local churches which mixed homogeneous units were more pleasing to God than those which ministered to only one homogeneous unit. Americans scolded themselves because "eleven o'clock Sunday morning is the most segregated hour in America." The whole thing created some terrible guilt complexes which at least partially account for the reason some oppose the church growth point of view so harshly today.

The debate is intense, the argument long, and the issue both crucial and unresolved. Many questions remain yet unanswered, but my own thinking as to why some resist the homogeneous unit principle so staunchly can be summed up as follows.

What Happened to Integration?

The residue of guilt produced by the blemish of outright racism and social injustice that has been and is yet perpetrated by some Anglo Americans on minority cultures hinders an objective consideration of the matter. It also prevents some from catching up with the times. Whereas integration and assimilation were being suggested as guiding principles for race relations in the early

1960s, they are no longer regarded as viable models today. Pluralism is a more acceptable model.

At the National Conference on Race and Reconciliation held in Atlanta in 1975, for example, none of the black evangelical leaders suggested integration as the wave of the future. They recognize that integration of a minority culture into a dominant culture will inevitably carry with it an undesirable assimilation of black culture into WASP culture. Now that black is regarded as beautiful, black leaders want to preserve black cultural values rather than sacrifice them in a process of social assimilation.

Regretfully, some who formed strong theological opinions on the matter of integration two decades ago are not yet ready to give them up, and these ideas tend to surface whenever the homogeneous unit principle is mentioned.

What Happened to the "American Dream"?

The second reason why I think some Americans resist the homogeneous unit principle is somewhat more subtle, but just as powerful. The myth that America is one big melting pot has had a pervasive influence on the American mentality. And it is now difficult for some to accept the fact that the "American dream" has never come true.

All recognize that America is a nation of immigrants, but some also suppose that a social chemistry called "Americanization" begins to operate when immigrants cross the borders and settle down in our land. In time, they are expected to become like "us Americans," usually defined as the white, middle-class kind of Anglo Americans. The dreamer of the American dream hopes that in a generation or two everyone in our country will have forgotten old differences and become like everyone else—all "Americans."

It is disappointing to those who feel guilty about the racist history of American whites and to those who still dream the American dream when they find out that diversity is on the *increase* in America. Instead of becoming more alike, Americans are progressively becoming more different. Immigration patterns indicate that dozens of minor ethnic groups are generating new internal strength around their ethnicity.

Some American Indians, for example, have given up on secularized technology and are now experimenting with a return to a simpler life-style more in harmony with nature. Many English-speaking adults are learning their tribal dialects as second languages. Black women who used to buy hair straighteners and skin lighteners now use a newer line of cosmetics that emphasizes the beauty of their blackness. Mexicans in California and Cubans in Florida are successfully demanding that their children be schooled in Spanish with English being taught only as a second language.

PLURALISM IS HERE TO STAY

What this all means is that America is a pluralistic society and probably will be forever. The great lesson that Americans have learned from the turbulent 1960s was that they must come to terms with pluralism. Our attitude ought not be that those different from us would be better off if they were more like us—that is properly labeled "cultural chauvinism." Our attitude, rather, should be that we recognize our cultural differences while respecting the cultural integrity of Americans different from us. And we should promote laws which will guarantee—much better than our present laws do—liberty and justice for all, not liberty and justice only for those who are most like "us," or who are most "American" according to our dream of what an American ought to be like.

Christians who are not comfortable with cultural pluralism and those who do not understand its full implications will continue to reject the homogeneous unit principle. They usually attack it as a denial of the doctrine of Christian unity and a return to racism and discrimination.

Racism Is Sin

It should be evident by now, however, that the homogeneous principle is just the opposite of racism. It is based on a high view of culture. It advocates the propriety of churches developing their Christian life-style in ways appropriate to the culture of their members.

The homogeneous principle opposes what some have called the "cultural circumcision" which is inevitable if those of one culture are forced to become Christians in a church of a different culture. It affirms the New Testament principle that Gentiles do not need to give up Gentile culture and adopt Hebrew culture in order to be accepted as the people of God. It is a modern day application of the decision of the Jerusalem Council reported in Acts 15.

It must be admitted, of course, that some churches are racist. Some white churches in America, for example, exclude blacks from membership. Some even forbid them from attending services. This is racism, and it must be condemned on biblical grounds.

Racism is sin and God hates it. So should His people. No church growth person that I know would advocate that a church be racist and exclude others because of their skin color or their foreign accent.

Now, having said this, we need to recognize that it is altogether possible for a church to develop basically within one homogeneous unit and still not be racist. I think my own church is one example.

Pasadena is a pluralistic community. The 1980 census lists 46 percent white, 21 percent black, 18 percent Hispanic and 15 percent other. Many of the whites are non-Anglo such as Armenians, Italians, Jews, Germans, etc.

We maintain the racial proportion in all our schools by busing children from one side of town to the other.

About half of my own neighbors are black. Day in and day out, we experience American social pluralism. Not that we have attained any ideal of social justice—we have a long way to go—but we keep trying and we make progress.

There are many fine Christian people in our community, some blacks, some whites, and some from other ethnic groups. For reasons easily understood according to the homogeneous unit principle, while black Christians and white Christians in Pasadena love each other in the Lord and while they consider each other on an equal plane as citizens of the Kingdom of God, when it comes to joining a local church most blacks prefer black churches and most whites prefer white churches.

Why?

Blacks say, "We've got soul."

Whites say, "We maintain dignity."

Lake Avenue Church is one of these dignified white churches. Not only is our homogeneous unit white, but it is accurately described by David Woodward as "predominantly middle and upper middle class white." However, it is not a racist church.

Any Christian at all who agrees with our philosophy of ministry and to whom our style of worship appeals is free to become a member of Lake Avenue Church with full standing. Something like thirty black families, twenty Hispanic families, sixty Filipinos, and many Koreans, Chinese, Armenians, Italians, and others belong to the church. Interracial marriages are received with open arms. My own Sunday School class includes most of the above in a loving fellowship group.

No one has taken a count, but there are also a considerable number of whites from the lower socio-economic levels and a few from the upper social class. Nevertheless, the homogeneous unit is clear and our entire church life-style is geared to meet the basic needs of this unit. This is one reason the church is growing.

Are there exceptions to the rule? Certainly. The homogeneous unit principle, like any other church growth principle, has exceptions. A limited number of churches are able to mix individuals from quite different back-grounds and grow well. But the people in those churches are ordinarily not nuclear ethnics, but rather marginal eth-nics who are in a process of mobility away from their origi-nal ethnic group or who are moving to middle or upper-middle class economic status. When such people congeal, frequently a new homogeneous unit forms. Earlier in this book I introduced Chapel Hill Harvester Church in Deca-tur, Georgia where blacks and whites freely mix. If I were to do an in-depth study of that church I would raise the question as to whether they are not seeing in their church and in their community the formation of a new homogene-ous unit.

Who Can Reach Archie Bunker?

As I was researching two churches in the Chicago area some years ago, I came across a fascinating contrast in homogeneous units. One was First Baptist, Hammond, Indiana and the other was Circle Church of Chicago. Each church had its defects, of course, but the strengths of each far outweighed its deficiencies. I saw both as fine exam-ples of contemporary American churches.

I was intrigued, however, to discover that the mem-bers in each church who were aware of the other had a very low opinion of each other. Though I doubt they meant it literally, some people in First Baptist Church questioned whether Circle Church members were really saved. And one or two people in Circle Church—certainly not those in leadership positions—were inclined to label Pastor Jack Hyles a heretic!

In my opinion, this very attitude was one of the defects of each of the churches. I don't think it would have occurred if each had been aware of and accepted the homogeneous unit principle. I hate to say it in so many words, because my friends in Circle Church get irritated when I do, but both are clearly homogeneous unit churches.

First Baptist is located in one of the most industrialized areas of America. A substantial part of the population of Hammond, Indiana is made up of blue collar workers and their families. As I met and talked to members of First Baptist, I found that a large number of them were shift workers who staff the factories and related services of the area.

First Baptist members are used to taking orders and working hard for a living. They are well dressed, but they have callouses on their hands, and many have dirt under their fingernails. The men wear their hair closely trimmed, and some have crew cuts.

Most of the First Baptist membership carry King James Bibles. And they paste patriotic bumper stickers on their cars. They are clearly a slice of middle America.

As I soaked up the atmosphere of First Baptist, it occurred to me that this is just the kind of church that could minister well to Archie Bunker, who was running on prime time television at the time. In fact, if Archie Bunker ever got converted, the odds are very high that it would be through the gospel preaching of a church just like this one. What a bus captain Archie would make if he only knew the Lord!

But I have serious doubts whether Archie Bunker would be attracted to a church like mine: too many beards and too few patriotic bumper stickers. Besides, Lake Avenue sold its last church bus some years ago.

Circle Church would be even less likely than mine to get an unconverted Archie Bunker to consider the claims of Jesus Christ. All he would need to make him look for the door would be one look at the blacks, the far-out dress, the elitist, liberal books on the booktable, the *Sojourners* and *The Other Side* for sale in the magazine rack, the dashikis, the long hair, and men wearing beards. Then if he heard the soul choir, the heavy social implications of the sermon (which he would probably interpret as "pinko"), the abstract level of conversation in the corridors, and the avant-garde worship format, he would disappear once and for all.

Circle Church was an interesting case study in itself because it was composed of a rather unusual homogeneous unit. Rather than being a unit determined by racial, linguistic or class difference—all of which are fairly evident when they are present—it was determined by psychological factors which may be invisible to the casual observer. The major factor welding Circle Church together was a liberal political stance. The life-style was very cause-oriented. The members, mostly educated on the college and graduate school level, mostly belonged to an intellectual elite. But, while this glue was sufficient to sustain the church for some years, it proved somewhat fragile. Ultimately the underlying cultural differences surfaced, and the black pastor left with the black members to form a new black church in the Austin district of Chicago. As they did, they announced that they preferred their "funky Jesus" to the "honky Christ," and suggested that the white members did not have enough concern for social justice.

WHY THE PRINCIPLE WORKS

To this point we have described homogeneous units and given some examples. The question now remains:

What makes them work? Why is it that churches made up of primarily one kind of people grow better than churches that mix different kinds of people?

It is important to keep in mind that the focus here is on evangelism, not Christian nurture. At this point some people get confused and mislocate the issue. They tend to forget that the basic question is, How can we establish an effective base for winning unsaved people to Christ? Instead they get sidetracked and ask, How should Christians show their love and fellowship for other Christians different from themselves? The first question has to do with evangelism, the second with Christian nurture.

If a given church decides to establish a philosophy of ministry around the principle of becoming a public showcase of socio-cultural integration, it can be done. After all, Christians are filled with the Spirit of Christ. In Christ there is no difference between Jew and Gentile or black and white. Bringing Christians from diverse cultures into a local fellowship will not be an easy job because it will require a degree of cultural circumcision on both sides, but with sufficient dedication, effort, and sacrifice, it can happen. However, when the task is completed, the resulting church will in all probability find itself rather limited as a base for effective evangelization in the future.

Some churches have actually found this to be the case, and they have theologized their lack of growth away. They feel that they reflect the true model of the Kingdom of God, they call their experiment "radical discipleship" and they are satisfied that God is smiling on their efforts even though they may not be winning many to Christ. It might well be that He is.

But too often such churches are scornful of other churches that have developed different philosophies of ministry, particularly those which are composed of a single homogeneous unit. They tend to say that the other church may be growing in quantity, but at the expense of the quality of a biblical gospel. They often accuse the other of dispensing "cheap grace."

The key question posed by the homogeneous unit principle is not how will Christians react to each other, but how will *unbelievers,* who know nothing of the Spirit of Christ, react to the preaching of the gospel when they hear it as they themselves perceive it? Church growth believes that evangelism is not completed with mere decisions, but that a true decision will be validated by responsible church membership.

There is no such thing as true commitment to Christ without commitment to the Body of Christ. Part and parcel of the preaching of the gospel should be the implication that those who accept it also join a local church. The church must not be something written in fine print or sneaked in afterwards when new converts are caught off guard.

If this is true, intelligent unconverted people, considering the claims of Christ will ask either outwardly or inwardly: "If I do this, what am I getting myself into? What kind of a group will I be expected to join?" So they take a look at the church.

Remember, they are not Christians. They know nothing of middle walls of partition, of Jews or Gentiles, of bond and free. It is natural for them to ask, "Are they my kind of people?"

If the answer is yes, they will be able at least to hear the gospel. But if the answer is no they may not even hear what is being proposed. In other words, Archie Bunker could be expected to hear the gospel from First Baptist, but less from Lake Avenue and even less from Circle Church. Accepting Christ must remain a religious, not a social or cultural decision.

Let's hope that if Archie Bunker ever became a Christian his bigotry and arrogance and selfishness would be transformed by God's Spirit into respect and humility and generosity. He would be a new creature in Christ. But there is no biblical requirement that I know of that would force him to violate either his own personality or his own culture. He would still prefer to identify with "my kind of people"—now of course "Christian people"—and join a church where he could feel at home. If he did so, he would be ever so much more likely to win his friends on the loading dock to Christ.

Judaizing and Gentilizing

Those who make changing culture a requirement to become Christian are called "Judaizers" in the Bible. In New Testament days, many people thought that the only people whom God would accept as bona fide members of His family were those who were circumcised, who kept the Sabbath, and who followed the Mosaic law. Many portions of the New Testament were written in the context of this problem since the Apostle Paul saw more clearly than some of the others that Gentiles could become Christians and still keep their Gentile culture.

It was as much a scandal to some in those days to think that Christians would continue to eat pork or go uncircumcised as it is to some today to think that Christians can drink wine or wear beards or vote Republican. So the Judaizers tried to put a stop to it, and wherever Paul went, telling Gentiles that they could have churches with their own Gentile life-style if they wanted to, they followed behind and told them that they'd better form Jewish style churches or else. They were ultimately condemned, of course, both in the Council of Jerusalem and in epistles such as Galatians and Ephesians.

An interesting reversal of this phenomenon has surfaced in our day. Within the last few years many of those involved in evangelizing the Jews have begun to apply the homogeneous unit principle with considerable success. They suddenly realized that the philosophy of what was called the "Hebrew Christian movement" was really a subtle form of modern-day gentilizing.

By suggesting that the normal thing for a converted Jew to do is to join a Gentile church, they were asking the Jew to commit cultural suicide. Through the years some did it, but not very many. The agony was so great that some Jewish families even held funerals for their family members whom they perceived as cultural traitors.

A few years ago, a number of workers deeply involved in Jewish evangelism became very much disturbed with the unfruitfulness of Jewish work through the years. Independently several of them came to a similar conclusion: The problem might be more *cultural* than *theological*.

Is there any way a Jew can believe in Jesus and still be culturally Jewish?

They knew from experience it couldn't be done very effectively in Gentile churches, so they developed what is now called "Messianic Judaism." The biblical model for their Christian community is Jerusalem rather than Antioch, so they don't even call themselves Christians. They prefer to be known as "followers of Jeshua Hamashiac," Jesus the Messiah.

They meet in messianic synagogues on Friday night rather than in Christian churches on Sunday. They circumcise their children and keep Kosher kitchens. They love Gentiles, and any Christian Gentile who wants to can join their synagogue—without being circumcised, but they make no mistake about it—their homogeneous unit is thoroughly Jewish.

Messianic Judaism will undoubtedly be a powerful evangelistic innovation. Synagogues which honor Jesus are springing up in Los Angeles, San Francisco, Florida,

New York, and other places. One reflection of the growing strength of the new movement was the change of the name of the sixty-year-old Hebrew Christian Alliance of America to the Messianic Jewish Alliance in 1975.

Basic Guidelines

What are the guidelines which emerge from the homogeneous unit principle?

Here is the first: *The social, racial, cultural, economic and linguistic composition of the local congregation should as nearly as possible reflect the corresponding marriage and family patterns of the community in which it exists if it is to maximize its evangelistic potential.* This honors the primary group relationships.

And the second: *In structures which are designed on a level over and above that of the local congregation, Christians should demonstrate practical ways and means of modeling their love and concern for those of other homogeneous units in a public way.* This promotes mixing people in secondary group relationships.

What does this mean in practice? It means that most small and medium churches, if they want to enjoy the maximum evangelistic effectiveness, do well to concentrate on the segment of the potential audience which they can best communicate with. No one church can reach everyone, as much as we would all wish it could. Therefore it is advisable to target the outreach on people who do not find it necessary to jump cultural barriers to accept Christ and join your church. This does not give any church license to turn anyone away from love, fellowship, support, or membership on the basis of race, color, social status, language, national origin, or culture. The homogeneous unit principle is not to be interpreted as exclusionary. Rather it attempts to see that the greatest possible number of individuals are included in the Kingdom of God by not erecting artificial barriers to the conversion experience.

Large churches can continue a strong growth dynamic, and at the same time include a wider spectrum of homogeneous units than can small or medium churches. This is usually done by creating within the large church a variety of congregations, as was explained in a previous chapter. In the congregations, and also in cells, church members tend to form primary group relationships with those of their own homogeneous unit. At the same time they enjoy the celebration and other all-church activities with brothers and sisters in Christ who differ from them in many ways, but who are bound together in love and mutual concern.

The Multi-Congregational Model

In some highly pluralistic communities such as inner cities, there may be a new and better way to relate the membership circle to the fellowship circle. A creative model has emerged under the leadership of Pastor James Conklin of Temple Church of Los Angeles. This church, located right in the heart of the city, is operating on what is called a "multi-congregational model." Within the church are several separate and semiautonomous congregations: Spanish, Korean, Anglo, Chinese, and potentially others.

Conklin, a veteran missionary from Thailand, has the oversight of the whole thing. The Spanish, Korean, and Chinese congregations each has its own pastor and lay leadership and congregational life-style. Conklin serves as pastor of the Anglo congregation. The cultural integrity of each is fully respected by the others. In order to avoid paternalism, each congregation contributes to the church budget according to the square footage of space used per week. Originally the Anglo congregation used the main sanctuary, but when the Spanish congregation outgrew it, the Anglo congregation had to move out of the main sanctuary and hold its services in a fellowship hall.

The congregations ordinarily worship separately, but on the first Sunday of each quarter a special celebration takes place called the "Sounds of Heaven." I have attended it and found it spectacular. It is a multi-colored, multi-cultural festival of music, rejoicing, baptisms, new members, sharing, and prayer. The congregational singing mixes four or more languages into the same tune and creates an uplifting cacophony of sound that may well reflect something of what heaven will, in fact, be like.

Notice that the way Temple Church does this is to create two levels of membership. Several smaller membership circles on one level obey the homogeneous unit principle. The total membership circle on the higher level promotes an enriching mixture of homogeneous units on a secondary group basis. The experiment is working well. It has outstanding potential for effective inner-city ministry.

Temple Church illustrates how the homogeneous unit principle can be used positively in an inner-city situation. But let's look next at another inner-city situation which helps us see how violating that same principle can have negative results in a similar urban setting.

STUDY QUESTIONS

1. What does the author say about a homogeneous unit? Discuss this as a group.
2. It has been said that America is a melting pot. It has also been said that the pot has not gotten hot enough. What is your feeling about a pluralistic society where people remain "unmeltable"?
3. Why is it that the homogeneous principle works in evangelism? Why the high priority of evangelism? Why is it necessary for a church to know its homogeneous units?

Chapter 9

THE AUTOPSY OF A DEAD CHURCH

Come with me into a church morgue. Here is a collection of corpses—churches that have recently died. They died of many different diseases. Some might have been cured if detected in time, some could never have been cured. In many of these cases their loved ones never knew what happened to them. There was no physician available when the symptoms became acute.

The "pathology of church growth," as this field might be called, is still a fairly young science. But those who have begun to concentrate on it are learning more and more about diagnosing the illnesses of churches and curing them with greater frequency. I have elaborated on this in considerable detail in my book, *Your Church Can Be Healthy* (Abingdon).

One of the techniques long used by medical science, but not too frequently by church leaders, is that of the autopsy. With some skillful slicing and testing, a dead body can provide much valuable information. Likewise, dead churches can offer clues that may save the lives of many others.

One of the problems with church pathology is that when a church's health begins to fail, the people who could best detect what is happening tend to abandon the patient. Top-flight pastors do not readily accept calls to dying churches. Denominational executives give higher priority to where the action is developing, not where it is decreasing. Religious editors of newspapers and magazines seek out success stories rather than examples of mediocrity or failure.

ETHNIKITIS: A SERIOUS DISEASE

So there are many corpses in this church morgue, but only a few of them have carried enough data to their death to be helpful to others. One of these which did is Zion Evangelical Free Church of Chicago. It died on August 31, 1969 of ethnikitis.

Not that I ever heard of "ethnikitis" before doing an autopsy on Zion Church, but the most obvious cause of Zion's decease was an ethnic problem. They were victims of metropolitan ethnic migration, otherwise known as a changing neighborhood. Studies have shown that ethnikitis is the chief killer of churches in the U.S.A. today.

As I write this I am looking at the graphs of eight Baptist churches of Birmingham, Alabama. In 1963 they had 2,405 in Sunday School. By 1973 the total had dropped to 161. Today all eight are dead—seven of ethnikitis.

Ethnikitis is caused by what are known as local contextual factors. That means sociological conditions in the neighborhood which are beyond the control of the local church. When a neighborhood church finds that its members are moving out of the neighborhood, when people of a different homogeneous unit move into the homes which they left, and when the church is an island of commuters in a neighborhood of people they are not equipped to minister to, the church has ethnikitis which is a terminal illness.

Unless God intervenes miraculously, the church will die.

In the previous chapter, I mentioned Circle Church in Chicago. Thanks to former Pastor David Mains, we do have a complete medical history of Zion Church. His book, *Full Circle* (Word Books), may not have been designed as a textbook on church pathology, but the information it contains is highly useful to put together an understanding of what took Zion to the grave.

In the late sixties and early seventies, Circle Church had gained a considerable measure of national recognition because of its highly nonconventional approach to some of the problems of an inner-city church. This had come about largely as a result of the creative leadership of its two principal staff members, David Mains (a white) and Clarence Hilliard (a black) who together attempted to model a harmonious interracial staff.

Mains, the founder of Circle Church, refused to be intimidated by such seemingly adverse inner-city conditions as a highly mobile society, great cultural diversities in the downtown area, changing neighborhoods, and the prohibitive costs of property. He built the membership of Circle Church around mobile people instead of sedentary people. Frequent farewells became a normal part of church life from the beginning.

A model called "the open church" was developed to accommodate believers of all races. The dress code that emerged was as permissive as possible. A black man who applied for a staff position, for example, made a favorable impression partly because he came to the interview dressed in a dashiki.

Established in 1967, Circle Church grew rapidly from an original 28 to 500 by 1970. The number then dropped to around 350 and plateaued at that level for some time. Approximately 120 of them were full, active members of the church body. One way they expressed their commitment was through participation in a number of small "mod-ules," which were task-oriented groupings of men and women who combined their spiritual gifts to accomplish a specific goal. The Circle Church story, which, because of David Mains's book, is familiar to thousands of Christians all over America, fairly bristles with valuable lessons for church growth, some positive and some negative.

The first positive lesson is a reinforcement of what we have said here about the first vital sign: the pastor has the power. David Mains is a person very uniquely prepared by God with a combination of spiritual gifts, personal trans-parency, and a heart for relating to people in a warm and supportive way. In the midst of the pressures and tensions that were part and parcel of contemporary inner-city life in Chicago, he was unflappable. At the same time, he is crea-tive and innovative, not intimidated by the risks involved in attempting new things for God. Very few people I know could have combined such qualities necessary for planting and nurturing a church like Circle.

A second plus was the development of the kind of cele-bration which met the needs of a significant group of peo-ple. The 1960s were the icy winter of the church in the U.S.A. Some were saying God was dead. Some were wishing the institutional church would die as well. Many, particularly the younger generation, were unable to relate well to the traditional stained glass and pipe organs and formality that they found in many churches.

But what they saw happening in Circle Church turned them on. Here was a vital Christian group praising God in new and dynamic ways. No two Sunday services were alike. The pastor seemed to be conversing with them instead of preaching at them. The musical mixture of soul and country and rock, combined with the more traditional, helped spice up Christian worship much to their delight. Scores of Christians, most of them under thirty, were attracted by the fresh style of Circle Church.

Another excellent move on the part of Circle Church avoided what some have called the "edifice complex." They could not afford a building, so they leased the Teamsters Union Hall which provided excellent facilities at a minimum cost. What's wrong with cleaning up the remains of Saturday night's beer party and worshiping God in the same place on Sunday morning? Since Circle Church economized on building expenses, they could use more of their budget on securing a quality staff, which they did.

The development of the module structure in Circle Church was also something that churches across the board should take a look at. By helping church members discover their spiritual gifts and then providing various task-oriented groupings through which they could corporately serve Christ, Circle Church was able to accomplish goals which would have been out of reach even in many much larger churches. It models a healthy form of decentralization as well as a good vehicle for lay liberation. For example, the Urban Module was deeply involved in the "Austin Project," designed to move Circle Church members into a depressed area of Chicago, largely black; to identify with the pains and problems of the community; to develop a holistic Christian ministry to youth, elderly, and others and to provide counseling, legal aid, health support, and higher quality education.

PEOPLE BLINDNESS: A SERIOUS HANDICAP

These and many other positive lessons for church growth emerge from the story of Circle Church. However, the principle reason for bringing Circle Church up at all in this chapter is to show how it relates to church pathology. In introducing Zion Church, I mentioned the disease called "ethnikitis." Circle Church suffered from a second kind of malady called "people blindness."

The term "people blindness" was popularized by Ralph Winter in his plenary session address at the International Congress on World Evangelization held in Lausanne, Switzerland in 1974. People blindness is not usually terminal, like ethnikitis, but it is a definite handicap. It blurs perception and, to different degrees, distorts reality.

People blindness comes from a failure to recognize the homogeneous unit principle of church growth. In its severe forms it can become cultural chauvinism. In its milder forms it simply results in a low view of cultural integrity. The Circle Church case is, I think, a mild one, but one that was fatal as far as Zion Church was concerned.

Back in those days the leadership of Circle Church refused to recognize itself as a homogeneous unit, and they became somewhat irritated when I suggested it was. But they were fair and open about our differences. I visited Circle many times, I talked privately to the pastors and the members, I met with modules, I was even invited to debate the subject with Pastor Clarence Hilliard from the platform on a Sunday morning.

Circle Church leadership believed that what they called the "open church" was the most biblical model of the Kingdom of God on the local church level. They interpreted the New Testament passages on the subject to mean that both Gentiles and Jews should meet together in local churches which are neither Jewish nor Gentile, but in which both cultures are respected. I once heard Hilliard interpret the Apostle Paul as saying, "The open church is not Gentile assimilation or loss of identity by absorption in an inadequate Jewish culture, but a mutual sharing through the cross of Christ of both Gentiles and Jews in the privileges and responsibilities of citizenship in God's new community in an atmosphere where differences are accepted and appreciated." I cannot fully agree with this interpretation, but I think it is an accurate statement of the position of Circle Church's leadership.

Circle Church leaders felt that because they had developed a multiracial church they had demonstrated the vulnerability of the homogeneous unit principle. In an *Eternity* magazine interview, Mains denied that Circle Church was a homogeneous unit in these words: "Our people differ racially, economically, sexually, politically, culturally, educationally, etc. Learning to love one another has been painful and the process is far from over, but we stand before our world testifying that the forces that would divide us are not as powerful as that which holds us together."

Almost as an aside, let me make one observation that may be pertinent. If Circle Church did turn out to be a true mixture of homogeneous units, this might have been one of the reasons why it did not grow well. The homogeneous unit principle is a vital sign of *growing* churches, not plateaued churches.

Of course, it may well be that, in the value structure of Circle leadership, it was more important to mix diverse people than to grow. It may be that Circle did not really want to grow. Mains did speak of their "small-church philosophy." And a church that does not want to grow should not be expected to grow.

As I analyzed this years ago, it still seemed to me that Circle Church was a homogeneous unit. I described the outward characteristics of that unit earlier when I contrasted it to Archie Bunker's kind of people. But later on I was able to label the homogeneous unit of Circle Church in a more accurate way, thanks to a neighbor of Circle Church, Andrew Greeley of the University of Chicago's Center for the Study of American Pluralism.

The title of one of Greeley's books articulates an attitude common to those who have people blindness: *Why*

Can't They Be Like Us? It is a book on America's *white* ethnic groups, showing how homogeneous units have been found in America without the distinguishing characteristic of different races. One of his chapters is entitled "Intellectuals as an Ethnic Group." When I read it, I found that he had identified and described Circle Church's homogeneous unit. Circle Church, I came to realize, was basically a church of *intellectuals* of all colors and all cultural backgrounds.

I remember holding a lengthy conversation with a young couple who had transferred membership from my own Lake Avenue Congregational Church to Circle Church. We discussed many similarities and contrasts between the two churches.

At one point the woman said, "In Lake the people our age would discuss common things like new recipes and how we were doing in raising our babies. But not in Circle. Almost every conversation deals with abstract concepts, new ideas, and philosophical or theological categories."

The comment fits in with Greeley's observation that intellectuals are a group set apart. He argues that it is most helpful in understanding the relationship of intellectuals to the rest of society "if we perceive that the intelligentsia is, in fact, an ethnic group."

Greeley helped me understand why I heard one or two people—not leaders—in Circle Church who wanted to label Jack Hyles a "heretic." Greeley, of course, is not writing about *Christian* intellectuals, but what he says fits fairly well. "The intellectual is quite capable of compassion," he says, "for the poor and the black, especially . . . but he is singularly selective in his compassion and in his willingness to understand sympathetically and defend members of other ethnic groups. He finds it difficult, if not impossible, to experience compassion or sympathy, or even understanding, for the United States of America and particularly for its middle-class and working-class citizens—especially if they are over thirty."

Greeley points out that the usual perjorative label pasted by intellectuals on middle Americans—like members of First Baptist, Hammond—who do not share their liberal political views is "fascists." "Heretics," I suppose, is a more religious version of the same feeling. And to turn the tables, the middle Americans in the secular world would likely label the intellectuals as "Commies," and Christians would probably make it "unsaved."

So, if intellectuals are an ethnic unit, they are vulnerable to ethnocentricity, just like the rest of the human race. Intellectuals ought to know better, but they also can be people blind, starting with not recognizing their own homogeneous unit. I may be wrong, but I perceive this to be at the root of two significant limitations connected with the outreach of Circle Church.

The first limitation relates to the evangelistic impotence of Circle Church in effectively evangelizing other important nearby homogeneous units. For example, the members of the Teamster's Union, whose hall Circle rented, were highly unlikely to consider the claims of Christ as presented to them by Circle members. Those who commuted to Circle Church from Wheaton—once voted an "All-American City"—found it very difficult to witness to their unsaved neighbors and persuade them to become Christians, if that implied joining a church like Circle. Unless, of course, their neighbors happened to be liberal intellectuals.

According to David Mains, one of the advantages presented by renting the Teamster's Hall was that they would bring an evangelical witness to the ethnic groups living in the immediate vicinity: ghetto blacks, skid row winos, Greeks, Puerto Ricans, and Appalachian or poor whites. Whereas Circle might have been in some vague sense a "witness," it was highly predictable on the homogeneous unit principle that new converts in any appreciable numbers would not be won from any of those groups into the Circle Church fellowship. The nearby Circle Campus of the University of Illinois provided an entirely different prospect: a large community of Circle Church's "kind of people" intellectuals. They could and did win them.

CIRCLE CHURCH AND ZION'S DEATH

The second limitation relating to Circle Church's outreach brings us back to where this chapter began. Circle Church's people blindness caused it to become the immediate cause for the death of Zion Church.

I say "immediate cause" because Zion already had ethnikitis before Circle Church came into the picture. Circle Church helped it die, but Zion was suffering from a terminal illness in the first place. Maybe, as it turned out, it was something like a mercy killing. A slower death might have been even more agonizing.

The Austin area of Chicago was at one time a white, middle-class neighborhood into which sufficient assimilating Scandinavians had moved to form an Evangelical Free Church. It had become a larger than average city church, around 350 in membership, and was drawing new members from the neighborhood which then contained people of the same homogeneous unit. But the racial upheavals of the 1960s brought rapid social change to Austin. A syndrome of white flight set in and the saints began marching from Zion. Within three or four years, Zion Church had dropped from 350 members to 30!

Terminal ethnikitis!

Those who stayed on were hearty saints of God. They were not about to let their church go without a struggle. They were desperate for help and ready to take almost anything that was offered.

Meanwhile, Circle Church had passed their planned optimum number of two hundred and were ready either to plant a new church or use their surplus membership to help some dying city church come back to life. They chose the latter, offered their help to Zion, and the offer was accepted. A contract was drawn up and signed on September 1, 1968, binding both parties to a one-year experiment.

For about a month signs of health began to return to Zion, as they often do to a terminal patient when one more artificial life supporting apparatus is attached to the body. But then, as Mains writes, "the cold, hard light of reality began to dawn." The patient began to fail rapidly.

The symptoms of mixing homogeneous units began to surface almost as inevitably as if a person with type A blood had received a transfusion of type B. The heaviest donor in the church left as soon as he heard that blacks would be welcome. A furor went up when some Circle girls showed up in miniskirts. An entire family left the church in protest when a songleader mounted the platform with long sideburns!

Not only did Zion members turn off to Circle members, but the reverse happened simultaneously. Many felt that Zion represented precisely what they had been liberated from. They couldn't stand the traditional church building, the moral legalism, the "stiff, rigid rows of pews"—as Anne Ortlund would say—the stained glass windows and the off-key organ. One or two visits was enough to convince them that they preferred to be with "our kind of people." They felt at home in Circle, but could not feel at home in Zion.

Once the final deterioration set in, death was inevitable. But the contract had been signed, and those involved doggedly stuck it out until the bitter end. On August 31, 1969, the contract terminated, and so did Zion Evangelical

Free Church. The next day the corpse was in the morgue; soon afterwards it was cremated. The empty building burned to the ground.

WHAT IS THE LESSON?

The purpose of a church autopsy is to learn something useful for church growth in the future. David Mains says that the greatest lesson they learned from the Zion experience was "that we cannot expect any place to be a carbon copy of Circle Church." This seems to me, however, to be only the beginning of the total lesson that needs to be learned.

Circle Church can reproduce itself, if it wants to, but *only* within its own homogeneous unit. There are dozens of groups of multi-racial intellectuals in American cities who would welcome a church with the Circle Church philosophy of ministry in their midst. Furthermore, although this homogeneous unit is not ordinarily among those most receptive to the gospel, there are probably thousands of unbelievers who would listen to the claims of Jesus Christ if they saw them backed up by a Christian community like Circle. There is considerable evangelistic potential here.

I consider it unfortunate that Circle Church eventually split on racial lines with Clarence Hilliard and the blacks moving out to the black area of Austin to start a new church. Apparently being black became a stronger unifying factor than being liberal or intellectual. This serves to reinforce even more strongly the main thesis of this chapter.

What we need to learn from this is simply that people blindness is a deterrent to effective evangelism. We need to respect the depth of human attachment to cultural values as a part of God's creation. We need to see the Christian implications of human diversity in a positive rather than a negative light.

We need to stop asking, "Why can't they be like us?"

We need to realize that American society is a fascinating mosaic of cultures and cultural subdivisions, and that members of each piece of the mosaic need liberty in Christ to develop the kind of a church where they can feel at home, and which will attract their friends to the Lord.

To the degree we accomplish all this, we will increase the potency of our evangelistic efforts, and our churches will be able to grow in a new way.

STUDY QUESTIONS
1. What are the characteristics of a church in a community with ethnikitis? Do you know of any such churches? What can be done to treat this serious church disease?
2. How do you feel about the author's description of Circle Church and its philosophy? Do you agree with his critiques? What is your perspective on his suggestion of a homogeneous unit?
3. How do you feel about the author's conclusion concerning Zion's death? Do you think he has proven his point? What do you think is the lesson to be learned here?

Chapter 10

DECISIONS OR DISCIPLES?

The sixth vital sign of a healthy, growing church is that it is using an evangelistic method that works.

Earlier I listed "ruthlessness in evaluating results" as one of the general characteristics of church growth people. If the goals are clear, if we have agreed that evangelism needs to be geared toward making *disciples,* not just decisions, then the methods are almost up for grabs.

CONSECRATED PRAGMATISM: METHODS THAT WORK

As I have studied growing churches in America, I have not struck upon any one method that is common to them all, or even to a significant number of them. For some churches a very effective method is bus ministry. Some grow by using house-to-house visitation, and many of them have developed their method around the Kennedy Evangelism Explosion model.

Others have found that a Christian parochial school has been a positive factor in evangelism. Still others have found the best approach is a drive-in church, the *Four*

Spiritual Laws, television broadcasts, neighborhood Bible studies—or a combination of these and many other methods.

To catalog the various methods that might work in your church or to evaluate one method against another would have minimal value here. Why? Because the right ingredients for your church's most effective method are as complex as the right ingredients for a pharmaceutical prescription. There is no such thing as a patent medicine that will cure all of the ills of man and beast, nor is there any universal method of evangelism that will help a church to grow.

As to the basic principle for discovering the proper method, though, I would have a hard time improving on Robert Schuller's maxim: *The secret of success is to find a need and fill it.* The methods used in growing churches, diverse as they might be, have all done this or they wouldn't be working. They have offered something which meets the needs of the kind of people they are ministering to.

At this point again the homogeneous unit principle is helpful. Every different homogeneous unit has a different set of needs. You will have a difficult time detecting people's needs if you do not know their homogeneous unit. Worse yet, if you don't, you might find yourself offering people solutions to problems they don't even have.

Whenever we imply that evangelistic methods are up for grabs, we are unashamedly recommending a fiercely pragmatic approach to evangelism. Likewise, it is a common mistake to associate pragmatism with lack of spirituality. Some are rightly afraid that pragmatism can degenerate to the point that ungodly methods are used, and this is not at all what church growth people advocate. The Bible does not allow us to sin that grace may abound or to use whatever means that God has prohibited in order to accomplish those ends He has recommended.

But, with this proviso, we ought to see clearly that the end *does* justify the means. What else possibly could justify the means? If the method I am using accomplishes the goal I am aiming at, it is for that reason a good method. If, on the other hand, my method is not accomplishing the goal, how can I be justified in continuing to use it?

Precisely at this point some evangelistic methods that have been used for years, even decades, need to be reevaluated. I fear that many have fallen into the trap of developing such outstanding programs with such well-oiled machinery, involving such substantial investments of time and money, that the program itself has become the end. The results, if evaluated at all, are evaluated very timidly.

A biblical proverb addresses this problem directly: "It is pleasant to see plans develop. That is why fools refuse to give them up even when they are wrong" (Prov. 13:19, *TLB*). When are plans wrong? Obviously, when they are not accomplishing the intended objective.

Our intended objective in evangelism and church growth is, we reaffirm, to make disciples. Bringing a person to a decision to accept Christ and to counsel and pray with that person is important as one of the means toward making a disciple. But if the person does not eventually make a commitment to the Body of Christ—usually validated by baptism and church membership, there is little to suppose that a disciple has been made.

If all a particular evangelistic method has been doing is to register decisions, it is hard to justify continuing it. Why? Because only accomplishing the *end*—making disciples—can justify the means.

THREE STREAMS OF EVANGELISM

I would like to bring this analysis into contemporary

focus by running briefly through the recent history of professional evangelism. As I perceive it, three basic streams of evangelism have been prominent over the past thirty years, with a new stream appearing each decade.

Crusade Evangelism

Crusade evangelism was characteristic of the 1950s and, of course, it continues today. It began to gain prominence with Billy Graham's Los Angeles crusade in 1949. The Billy Graham Evangelistic Association was formed in 1950 and, for at least a decade, holding a city-wide crusade was almost universally considered the most effective evangelistic method.

The crusade involved organizing a local committee of Christian leadership in a given city, enlisting the cooperation of as many churches as possible, encouraging broad prayer support, training large united choirs and counseling teams, contracting a stadium or some other public meeting place, advertising the crusade as widely as possible, and then inviting the evangelist and his team in for a given number of days. When the evangelist was through, the task of follow-up was then undertaken by the pastors of the local churches that had cooperated.

Crusade evangelism was criticized by the extreme right and the extreme left for different reasons, but mainline evangelicals fairly well accepted it as a good evangelistic method. Surprisingly little was done in an attempt to evaluate the method against the results. One of the reasons for this was that during the 1950s evangelicals were self-consciously attempting to carve a more prominent niche for themselves in American religious life, and the one evangelical who had attained the highest status as a religious leader in America also happened to be the evangelist Billy Graham. Consequently, few evangelicals in America were in the mood to apply fierce pragmatism to crusade evangelism in the 1950s.

But one person outside America was not so timid. He was Kenneth Strachan of the Latin America Mission, whose father, Harry Strachan, was the most prominent crusade evangelist in Latin America for some time. As Strachan took a long look at crusade evangelism, he began to raise questions about what I now call the "follow-up gap." This is the difference between the number of people who register decisions and the number of those who can finally be counted as disciples. In other words, Strachan noticed that in too many cases there was a great deal of evangelistic zeal and activity, but little church growth as a result.

Saturation Evangelism

Strachan set about correcting the method. In his opinion the basic fault of crusade evangelism was too much dependence on the outside evangelist and too little dependence on the people of the local churches. His answer was the program of total mobilization described earlier.

Strachan knew that the people could not be mobilized without first mobilizing the pastors, and it soon became evident that more time was needed than for the typical crusade. He developed a year-long nationwide program and called it "Evangelism in Depth." This concept quickly rose to prominence in evangelical circles, particularly outside of the U.S.A. Throughout the 1960s it became known as "saturation evangelism" and was a very widely accepted method. It came to America in 1973 under the program of Key 73.

Toward the end of the decade, a few researchers began asking the kind of questions about Evangelism in Depth that Strachan—by this time with the Lord—had asked about crusade evangelism. With all the additional time, effort, prayer, and money being invested in this evangelistic method, had it really solved the problem of the follow-up gap?

As the results of rather extensive research were compiled over a period of time, it was found that the follow-up gap was still there. Saturation evangelism had many other positive effects on Christian people, but it did not pass the test of fierce pragmatism as far as evangelism was concerned.

Body Evangelism

A new effort was begun in the 1970s to solve the nagging problem of the follow-up gap. It has its roots in the church growth movement and the principles it uses are based on church growth philosophy. For most of the decade of the seventies the chief worldwide advocate of what is being called "body evangelism" was Vergil Gerber of the Evangelical Missions Information Service. From his Wheaton, Illinois base, Gerber moved into more than fifty countries holding church growth workshops and sharing the concept of body evangelism.

The major innovation of body evangelism is not that it proposes a method that might be substituted for crusade evangelism or saturation evangelism, but that it helps clarify the goal against which any method must be ruthlessly evaluated. The goal is church growth, and students of body evangelism are taught that if a particular method does not contribute to the growth of Christ's church, it should be discarded as quickly as possible.

The principles of body evangelism were tested in a controlled two-year experiment among over forty churches in Venezuela, in which I had the privilege of participating. The decadal growth rate of the churches increased from 60 percent to 250 percent over those two years. No guarantee is being made for such dramatic rises in rates of church growth, of course, but as the body evangelism mentality grips missionaries and pastors and evangelists, old methods are being called into question when they do not help churches to grow. An attitude of fierce pragmatism is growing worldwide.

This kind of pragmatism is also *consecrated* pragmatism. It is a biblical attitude. For one thing, it measures evangelistic methods against biblical goals, namely the Great Commission imperative to make disciples of all nations (see Matt. 28:19). For another it takes seriously the notion of shaking the dust off the feet if results are not forthcoming under certain circumstances (see Matt. 10:14).

It incorporates the attitude of the owner of the barren fig tree when he found that the tree should have been bearing fruit but was not. "Cut it down," he said. "Why does it use up the ground?" (Luke 13:7). It avoids the foolishness addressed in Proverbs 13:19 when a person can delight in the development of a program, even when it is wrong.

AN AUTOPSY OF KEY 73

It is generally conceded that America's great attempt at a nationwide program of saturation evangelism, Key 73, did not live up to expectations. Perhaps another autopsy is in order.

Why did such a promising evangelistic method fizzle?

I have read several post-mortems on Key 73, but none has completely satisfied me. Some have avoided the ticklish question of what went wrong and dealt only with what went *right.* It is generally recognized that three things in particular went right with Key 73:

1. Scripture portions were distributed in unprecedented numbers.

2. Home Bible study and prayer groups for Christians multiplied and strengthened the faith of many.

3. New levels of cooperation among Christians were reached.

The Key 73 program touched upwards of 100 thousand American congregations, but without any noticeable change in patterns of growth across the board. I was fearful of this and beforehand I pled for the introduction of sound church growth measuring instruments so that the evangelistic effectiveness of Key 73 could be accurately assessed in the years to come.

In a *Christianity Today* article I said, "It would be a shame to 'spend many long hours in prayer, interaction, study and research in trying to sort out strategy, materials, methods, and suggestions which we feel can be most effectively used in a great evangelistic thrust for our nation,' as the *Key 73 Resource Book* suggests, and when it is all over, not be able to look back and accurately report whether the effort was a success or failure." And just because no such feedback mechanism was developed, it is not easy now to put a finger on precisely what went wrong with Key 73.

It is not a total mystery, however. I have spent a good bit of time on the Key 73 autopsy and have concluded that there was a two-fold problem:

The first had to do with *the basic concept of evangelism.* Evangelism was interpreted as proclamation of the gospel rather than as persuading people to become followers of Jesus Christ and responsible members of local churches.

The second basic problem with Key 73, however, relates more directly to the theme of this chapter: *the methods of evangelism.*

Hyper-Cooperativism

If, as a result of the autopsy on Key 73, I were to add a third growth-inhibiting disease to ethnikitis and people blindness, I would call it "hyper-cooperativism." While some cooperation may be good as a method to accomplish certain Christian goals, if it is overdone it can kill evangelistic efforts such as Key 73. In the same way, I believe, too much cooperation was one of the debilitating elements of Evangelism in Depth, and further research tends to reinforce my earlier observation.

The point is controversial, so much so, in fact, that a reviewer friend of mine believed I wrote with tongue in cheek when I suggested in one of my older books that Evangelism in Depth went overboard on its principle of "visible unity of the body of Christ." The verse, "That they all may be one . . . that the world may believe that You sent Me" (John 17:21), has been made to mean too much if it is taken as a contemporary guideline for evangelistic methods.

The danger is that such an interpretation can lead to a false hypothesis, namely that the more cooperation Christians attain, the more effective will be their evangelistic efforts. Those who accept this hypothesis often tend to confuse priorities. Evangelism slips, sometimes unnoticed, from the top of the priority list and cooperation takes its place. Cooperation, then, becomes an end in itself instead of a means to the end of effective evangelization.

In the whole development of the Key 73 idea, for example, the generating influence was an editorial in *Christianity Today* (June 9, 1967), entitled "Somehow, Let's Get Together." The text mentioned the "debilitating restraints of conciliar ecumenism" and lamented the "fragmented fringes of independency," suggesting that evangelicals take the middle road and fulfill their longing for "dramatic new dimensions of fellowship across denominational lines." The central thrust of this long and tightly-argued editorial was cooperation. Evangelism was mentioned two or three times, but only in passing.

Response to the editorial was very positive. Evangelicals said in a loud voice that they did want to cooperate with one another. But how? After a few consultations, it became evident that one of the major areas where cooperation could most likely succeed was that of evangelism.

Key 73 was then adopted as a program which could serve as an instrument for evangelicals "somehow getting together." So without anyone's intending it at all, evangelism was used as a means to the end of cooperation. The effort was referred to as *cooperation for evangelism,* but deep down it was more realistically *evangelism for cooperation.*

What a mistake! The liberal magazine, *Christian Century,* saw it clearly when it commented in early 1974, "Although Key 73 was labeled an evangelistic effort, its uniqueness lay in its *ecumenical character.*"

Blurring the Focus on the Local Church

One of the major problems with cooperation as an evangelistic method is that it tends to remove the central focus from the local church. *If effective evangelism happens it has to begin and end with the local church,* and all that is involved in large cooperative efforts can be distracting.

As I look across America and see growing churches, all of which have developed successful evangelistic methods of one kind or another, I do not know of many which attribute their evangelistic success to cooperation with other local churches. Each one realizes that there is no way that one system of evangelism can meet needs across the board any more than there is a patent medicine that will cure all ills. The more that evangelistic methods are tailor-made for each local church, the more likely they are to contribute to local church growth.

I recall working with my good friend Albert Runge, who then was pastoring the North Avenue Alliance Church

of Burlington, Vermont, on an analysis of his church
growth some time ago. His church was then growing at a
rate of 644 percent per decade and had planted a daughter
church some years previously. As he studied the fluctua-
tions in annual growth rates, he noticed that the rate for
one year was far and above that of the years just before
and just after. After a few minutes of reflection, light came
to his eyes. "That was the only year," he exclaimed, "that
we decided not to go in with the other churches on a city-
wide evangelistic program, but to have our own local
church evangelistic program!"

The point I want to make is not that cooperation is a
bad thing or that it is wrong for churches to cooperate. But
if the kind of cooperation we have assumed to be a help to
evangelism over the past few years actually turns out to
be a hindrance, consecrated pragmatism says get rid of it
and try something that will in fact bring people to Christ
and into responsible church membership. It could well be
that we have yet to discover new ways of cooperation that
will help make evangelism more effective. But if we sanc-
tify the past forms and place them on a pedestal beyond
the range of criticism, we will not even begin to look for
the new forms.

Another one of our larger evangelistic organizations
once approached me indirectly and asked for suggestions
as to how the evangelistic impact of a fine new Christian
film could be made more effective in cities across the
nation. They had already worked out a system of getting
decisions registered on cards. How could more of these
decisions become disciples?

I'm afraid my answer was slightly too radical for them,
since I suggested that they might need less, rather than
more, cooperation from local churches. It occurred to me
that in the average city there are many churches that,
even if they received a stack of valid blue chip decision

cards from people who had been born again, they would
not be qualified to attract these people into membership.
They are static churches and exhibit all the negative characteristics of stagnation. New believers would need only
one exposure to the dull atmosphere, the puny attendance, the boring worship service, the gloom on the faces
of many of the members and the negative thinking that
often comes through to decide that they want no part of
that kind of a church.

There are usually other churches in the same city,
however, that even before the film comes, are well prepared to absorb new believers. How could they tell the difference?

I suggested that they restrict the churches which are
allowed to cooperate with them and receive decision cards
to those which can demonstrate an annual growth rate of 5
percent or more. This figures to a decadal rate of 63 percent. Most churches at that level are in better shape to
minister to new believers than those growing at a lesser
rate. That move in itself would narrow the follow-up gap.

Another way to do it would be to promote competition
rather than cooperation. I wonder what would happen if
the whole system were set up and publicized so that copies of each decision card were given to several churches at
once. Then they could rush the person who made the decision like fraternities rush freshmen on college campuses.
May the best church win! If nothing else, it would make
new believers feel they were wanted, and give them more
than one option as to where they wanted to make a long-
term commitment.

I have no idea whether the above suggestions are
workable methods. What I do know, however, is that they
can't be much *worse* than methods used previously in city-
wide evangelistic efforts. I am simply illustrating in a relevant way the kind of mentality that is necessary for opti-

mum church growth. For, whatever the cost, we must be prepared to discard old methods that have not worked and introduce new ones that do work if we are serious about world evangelization.

STUDY QUESTIONS

1. How would you go about discovering the best method of evangelism in your community? Name several ways and discuss it as a group.
2. What's your reaction to the contrasting of body evangelism and crusade evangelism? Do you feel that your church could be effective in body evangelism? If so, where would you start?
3. Has your church set a goal for evangelism this year? What is it? If not, why not? Is that goal persuasion centered? If not, why not?

Chapter 11

ARE YOUR PRIORITIES IN ORDER?

The seventh—and last—vital sign common to healthy, growing churches in America is that they have their priorities straight. Such churches have come to realize, either intuitively or analytically, that the most important function their church has in its community is a *religious* function.

Throughout his landmark book, *Why Consecrated Churches are Growing,* (Harper and Row), Dean M. Kelley deals with the matter of priorities. What are churches for? What do people in an average American community expect of a church?

Dean Kelley, a sociologist of religion who works not for conservative churches but for the National Council of Churches in New York City, comes through loud and clear. In his opinion, the one indispensable function of the church in America is to explain the meaning of life to people in ultimate terms.

WHAT DO PEOPLE NEED?

People are hungry for many things. They are hungry for food, for employment, for more adequate housing, for recreation, for financial security, for good health, for more stable marriages, for companionship, and for God. Churches can, and do, help meet all those needs to one extent or another. In all of them but one, however, they are aided and supplemented by other social institutions, some government and some private.

The one acute human need that churches and *only* churches can meet is the desire to relate to the ultimate, to know God personally. In plainer biblical language, churches are places where people can be saved. No other social institution can match that claim.

Churches may choose to major in functions other than bringing people to God. They may desire to become model agencies for social reform, for example. Certainly there is nothing at all wrong with social reform as a legitimate Christian activity. But to the degree churches allow it to become the top priority in their church life, they will find that their potential for growth is reduced.

The pastors of the growing churches I have studied knew this fact of life before Dean Kelley wrote his book. Their top priority has always been to bring lost men and women, alienated from God by sin, into reconciliation to Him through the blood of Christ. Gospel preaching is the most important thing they do. They are not indifferent to the social ills around them, but most of them have long since come to realize that God did not call them to be political activists or social engineers. God called them to be pastors, shepherds of the flock, and they cannot be faulted for giving their pastoral function top priority.

Typically, pastors of growing churches avoid even mentioning the burning social issues of the day in their pulpits. In one of his lectures, Robert Schuller straightforwardly advises pastors not to be controversial from the pulpit. "In controversy," he says, "you may relieve your frustration, and you will certainly earn enough opposition to boast that you are 'being persecuted for righteousness sake.'" He warns, however, that in almost every instance to engage in controversy will do the cause more harm than good.

This same attitude is roundly condemned by many other pastors today, particularly by those who received their seminary training during the 1960s, the heyday of social activism. Many of them have since modified their attitudes to keep up with the times, but some would still rather lead their church into a posture of what they consider to be social relevance, even if they know ahead of time that their church may decline in numbers if they do so. I was recently in a social action-oriented church where the pastor believed so strongly in preaching on social issues that he caricatured others as promoting "home-on-the-range churches" where "never is heard a discouraging word"!

Predictably, his church is not growing, but this is of little concern to him. What he and many others like him have yet to learn is precisely the major finding of Dean Kelley's research: Churches that concentrate on developing a philosophy of ministry around social activism tend, in the long run, to *lose* social strength. This is ironic, since the intentions of socially-oriented pastors are just the opposite: They would love to change the world. But the frustration level in churches like this is frequently high because it usually doesn't turn out that way. Dean Kelley himself says that he would be delighted if his thesis were disproved, but "it will take more than insistence to disprove it." He says that he has searched for twenty years for just one case which would disprove the theory, but has not yet found it.

What about liberal churches? In his book, Kelley explains sociologically why liberal churches are not growing. He points out that all social organizations offer what could be likened to a menu for the general public. It contains a presentation of the offerings intended to attract people to join that particular organization.

Many liberal churches will offer art or music appreciation, instruction in women's liberation, guidelines as to which political causes to support at a given time, dialogues with important community leaders, marches to protest nuclear energy, and other such activities. But if this is the menu the church offers, few people are interested.

Why? Because the competition in these areas is too keen. Ours is a free society where people can choose what they will join and what they will not. And since almost anyone can find equal or better opportunities for political, social, or academic involvement in secular organizations than most liberal churches can deliver, they reject the menu and choose not to join.

"Conservative churches, on the other hand," Kelley goes on to say, "offer an incentive (or commodity?) that is not widely available—salvation—and offer it persistently."

And what about some conservatives? Admittedly, not all conservative churches are growing either. Kelley, and everyone else, knows this. We have all seen or belonged to rock-ribbed conservative churches which show all the signs of strictness and which persistently offer salvation, but which are dead on the vine.

But all this only reminds us that church growth is a complex matter. If a church declares that saving souls is its top priority, but violates a half-dozen other church growth principles, it cannot expect to grow. So a better title for Kelley's book might have been *Why Liberal Churches Are Not Growing,* because there are precious few examples of churches which violate this particular church growth principle of first things first and which continue to grow.

Can growing churches serve, too? Contrary to what some would suspect—or even hope, the measurable social good that is being accomplished by growing, conservative churches probably far exceeds that of their liberal counterparts. Since liberal churches rather consistently lose social strength, their practical contribution to social change often becomes tokenism. A manifesto here, a contribution to a labor union there, some signatures on a petition, a headline or two, a poor family helped back on its feet—all commendable activities—but year after year there is little that really makes much difference. If the number of members continues to decline, the resources will also decline, and even less will be possible than before.

When a church is growing, however, and when large numbers of people are excited about giving themselves and their resources to serving God in all ways, a great deal can be done. Take, for example, the First Baptist Church of Hammond, Indiana, a church which is showing most of the vital signs of a growing church. Over an extended period of time the growth in Sunday School attendance—the one statistic that seems most significant to Pastor Jack Hyles—maintained a decadal rate of over 400 percent. The average attendance is around 18 thousand, and on one Sunday the attendance in Sunday School topped 101 thousand, a national record. A total of 74 thousand names are on the church roll.

There is no question about priorities at First Baptist. Even a casual visitor would immediately learn that the church feels its primary responsibility is soul-winning. Hyles says, "The soul-winning fundamental churches are the only hope of America. I want to build a New Testament church that can be reproduced all over America to help save our nation."

One could easily conclude, and many do, that this kind of language reflects an overly narrow view of the whole person. Hyles has frequently been accused of treating people as if they didn't have social as well as spiritual needs. He has heard it many times, and he has this to say: "Our primary aim is to win souls; any social work we do is secondary." Then he continues. "Our church does more social work secondarily than most liberal churches do primarily."

This has been substantiated across the board by some research done by the Gallup Organization. They set out to determine which churches were most involved in social service activities. Forty-two percent of evangelical Christians were personally involved as compared to only 26 percent of nonevangelical Christians.

Helping the Handicapped

Seeking out and ministering to the handicapped is one of the ways the people of First Baptist show their compassion for some of the less fortunate people of society. By identifying with the deaf, the blind, and the educable slow, they are relating to the outcasts of American society in a way reminiscent of how Jesus related to the outcasts of His day.

For example, there are 14 million deaf in the United States today. Theirs is a lonely world. They feel that those who can hear generally misunderstand, ridicule, pity, and even ignore them. Their fellowship on any meaningful level is restricted to other deaf with whom they can communicate in sign language. Less than 1 percent of deaf people outmarry. Very few churches have developed the professional skills, the attractive program, or the staff to meet their needs in any significant way.

At the last count I have, 600 deaf were enrolled in the deaf program of First Baptist in thirty-one different classes. One of the challenges kept before the hearing people of the church is to participate in Christian service by becoming a trained deaf interpreter. Here is the challenge as expressed in a church instruction manual: "As an interpreter you will, no doubt, interpret in the doctor's office, lawyer's office, courtroom, and hospital; for funerals and weddings; in finding employment for them, etc. It may become hectic but it is never dull. May the Lord give you wisdom as you labor for Him with the 'overlooked' people in your home town and area."

Educating Educable Slows

Few of the ghetto dwellers in the darkest inner cities of our country are as severely alienated by society as the mentally retarded. And few people of any color have taken up their cause with zeal. Since they are incapable of writing articles or marching through streets or burning buildings, they have not been able to launch a liberation movement for themselves like many of our other minorities have. They number six million, so they constitute a considerable segment of American population.

The educable slows are another group of needy and oppressed people that First Baptist has compassionately related to. Under the supervision of well-trained personnel, 450 educable slows receive the love, care, and fellowship of persons who give themselves in the spirit of Christ, expecting no reward whatsoever except from their Lord. Ten closely graded Sunday School classes have been designed and staffed to help meet their needs.

And there is more! Once the deaf and mentally retarded programs were moving in First Baptist, a similar one was started for the blind. They now minister to twenty-five adult and teenaged blind. The church also distributes numerous free hot meals to the poor each week, collects and distributes clothes, and provides food baskets and money to families in need.

A full-time staff member is assigned to shut-ins and handicapped. The church operates the Hammond Rescue

Mission to minister to the destitute of the city. Plans are on the drawing board for a senior citizen housing complex and an orphanage.

Illustrations do not have to be multiplied to further substantiate the point that because growing churches put their spiritual responsibility first, many of them are able to exercise their material and social responsibilities in a greatly expanded and highly relevant way.

THREE BIBLICAL PRIORITIES

No one I know has worked out the biblical principles for setting priorities better than Raymond Ortlund. While he was pastor of Lake Avenue Congregational Church he made sure that every member understood the "three priorities": (1) commitment to Christ; (2) commitment to the Body of Christ; (3) commitment to the work of Christ in the world. They are used so frequently around the church that to refer to "Priority One" or "Priority Two" is as common and mutually understood as "choir practice" or "missionary committee."

The promotional brochure given out to first-time visitors lets them know that these priorities were "in cement." In other words, even before joining a membership class, people were informed as to what the church was all about. Then as a requirement for membership they all read Ortlund's best-seller, *Lord, Make My Life a Miracle* (Regal), which explained the priorities in detail. No surprises after the fact!

Priority One

Raymond Ortlund interprets Matthew 6:33 literally: "Seek *first* the kingdom of God and His righteousness, and all these things shall be added to you" (italics added). There is nothing that can substitute for relating to God and to Jesus Christ as Lord as the *first* step in the Christian life. If people have not become new creatures in Christ, if they are not in touch with the Holy Spirit, if their life-style is not a constant walk with God, they are not prepared to fulfill Priority Two or Priority Three. Christians must live from the center out, and the center is God.

Priority Two

The second priority is second only in order, not importance. These are not three *options* from which Christians may pick and choose. Christian life is incomplete without all three operating in harmony.

For these priorities to make a difference in your life, however, it is necessary for you to understand their precise order. There is no way to start with Priority Two or Priority Three and work back. Priority One is first, but if it does not lead through decisively to Priorities Two and Three, it can and will go sour.

Priority Two is stated like this: "We are committed to each other in Christ. We are called the Body of Christ. So we are connected and made to be dependent on each other in His Body. That means we must love and care for each other."

Those committed to this philosophy of ministry believe that there is something phony and unbiblical about people who claim a relationship to God but who do not commit their lives in love to other Christian people. The Bible has too much to say about Christians being members of a Body to give much credibility to the person who says, "My church is out there beside a babbling brook on the hillside."

Unless Christian people put it all together and model love, concern, generosity, and sacrifice among themselves, they will not be well prepared to share with those who are not yet Christian. God's Word tells us that as we have opportunity we should do good to all people, but "especially to those who are of the household of faith" (Gal. 6:10). "By this all will know that you are My disciples," Jesus said, "if you have love for one another" (John 13:35). Loving one another, starting with the nuclear family and spreading to all the people of God, is Priority Two.

Priority Three

Priority Three is the work of Christ in the world. Not only does the Bible instruct Christians as to how they should relate to one another, but it also gives them some commands as to how they should relate to those who are not yet Christians.

These commands are clustered around two major focal points which are called different things by different people. Jack Hyles calls them "soul-winning" and "social work." Theologians refer to them by the Greek words, *kerygma* and *diakonia*.

My colleague, Arthur Glasser, has popularized the terms *evangelistic mandate* and *cultural mandate*. Others have described them as the vertical dimension and the horizontal dimension, or redemption and humanization.

EVANGELISM AND SOCIAL INVOLVEMENT

Not that the words matter much, but I like to describe these two focal points as "evangelism" and "social involvement." Both are part of Priority Three. Both need to be done if the Christian is to model commitment to the work of Christ in the world.

As far as I can tell, the leadership of every growing church in America would affirm their agreement with this. But they also know something more than this. They know that within Priority Three is a set of subpriorities. They consistently give evangelism the priority over social involvement, even though they attempt to do both.

To go back to Lake Avenue Congregational Church for

a moment, here is how Priority Three is explained: "We are committed to the work of Christ. We want this world to know the Saviour who died for all. It makes no difference what color or age or social status or nation.

"We crave to tell everyone that 'God so loved the world that he gave his only begotten son!' God thinks all people are worth that! That's good news! That's the gospel!"

Notice that the stress is on evangelism. Nothing appears in this context about social involvement. If what Dean Kelley has discovered is valid, this is exactly what a church brochure designed for the general public should stress.

People expect the church to say something important to them about the ultimate meaning of life. Christians know that this involves relating to God through Jesus Christ, and call it evangelism.

Prioritization of Evangelism

I must admit at this point that there is no general agreement among evangelicals—to say nothing about liberals—that evangelism should take priority over social involvement. In fact, this was one of the most hotly debated issues at the 1974 International Congress on World Evangelization in Lausanne, Switzerland, and it remains a point of contention on the Lausanne Committee of which I happen to be a charter member. Several evangelicals at first refused to sign the *Lausanne Covenant* because they could not agree with what they call the "prioritization of evangelism."

This is what the *Lausanne Covenant* says about Priority Three: "We affirm that Christ sends his redeemed people into the world as the Father sent him, and that this calls for a similar deep and costly penetration of the world. We need to break out of our ecclesiastical ghettos and permeate non-Christian society. In the church's mission of sacrificial service *evangelism is primary*" (Article 6).

I heartily agree with this section of the Covenant and sign it without reservation. I was delighted that such a prestigious gathering of Christians from around the world affirmed the prioritization of evangelism as a church growth principle. It was later reaffirmed in the Consultation on World Evangelization held in Pattaya, Thailand in 1980. Nothing is more important for a church that wants to grow than to make as the first item of its message to those without: "We are ambassadors for Christ, as though God were pleading through us: we implore you in Christ's behalf, be reconciled to God" (2 Cor. 5:20).

Evangelism, of course, includes local evangelism as well as worldwide missions. Both are essential elements of Priority Three. Both are inescapable Christian obligations.

Social Involvement Needs Planning

The second subpriority in doing Christ's work in the world is social involvement. Though I have yet to discover a close correlation between the degree of social involvement and the growth rate of the church, on biblical principles alone I firmly believe in it.

Jesus gave us the example. He healed the sick. He cleansed lepers. He ate with publicans and sinners. He fed the hungry. He cast out demons. He identified with the poor and outcast while at the same time He loved Roman centurions and government tax collectors.

Many Christians make the mistake of thinking that Priority Three will happen spontaneously if they just do well enough on Priorities One and Two. Experience shows that it will not just happen. Effective evangelism usually is a result of planning as well as prayer.

Just because a church is evangelizing well there is no

assurance that it will automatically do a good job of social ministry. I cannot agree with the oversimplification that goes: "Saved souls will change society." All too much evidence shows that they often do not.

Many growing churches have little or no social ministry and unfortunately this turns some people against the whole church growth philosophy. I think such people throw the baby out with the bathwater, but I applaud their efforts to joggle socially uninvolved churches out of their lethargy.

Some growing, evangelical churches are not more socially involved because they don't quite know how to handle the situation. On one hand, they want to do something, but on the other they don't want to do the wrong thing. They are aware of such incidents as the contribution of the United Presbyterian Church to the fund for a fair trial for Angela Davis and the devastating effects of that action on the denomination ever since. They dread the thoughts of making the same mistake.

Evangelicals don't want to fall into the trap that Dean Kelley warns so clearly against. They read books like David Howard's *Student Power and World Evangelization,* learn that a powerful evangelistic organization like the Student Volunteer Movement went under chiefly because social involvement eventually gained priority over evangelism, and they don't want the same thing to happen to their churches.

Social Service vs. Social Action

One clue to the evangelism/social involvement dilemma is found in the distinction between the concepts of *social service* and *social action.*

Social service is designed to relieve immediate needs of people: healing the sick, feeding the hungry, clothing the naked, counseling the emotionally disturbed, finding work for the unemployed, and so on.

Social action is something else. It makes the more radical demand to change the structures of society so that the poor and oppressed will get a fairer piece of the social pie, so to speak. Social action ordinarily involves politics of some kind or other. It requires joining parties, forming pressure groups, signing petitions, making public declarations, getting out voters, and even in some cases outright revolution.

How should churches, as distinguished from Christians as individuals or in groups, relate to social problems according to this classification? I would suggest here a sub-subpriority under social involvement. If churches are going to develop a social ministry (and I think they should), they will do well if they stick to social service and leave social action to other organizations, both secular and Christian.

Though I have not detected a relationship of social involvement to church growth, let me articulate here a related principle: *To the degree that socially involved churches become engaged in social action, as distinguished from social services, they can expect church growth to diminish.*

You will know of some exceptions to this rule. Black churches which are traditionally deeply involved in social and political issues are an example. But the key to the exceptions is harmony in the congregation. If taking a stand on a given political issue causes controversy in the local congregation, it will retard growth. If it is agreed upon, such as a stand against abortion in a conservative church, it will not hinder growth. I have elaborated on this important issue in great detail in my book *Church Growth and the Whole Gospel* (Harper and Row).

With this principle established, we can outline now the biblical priorities which constitute the seventh vital sign of healthy, growing churches.

Priority One: Commitment to Christ.
Priority Two: Commitment to the Body of Christ.
Priority Three: Commitment to the work of Christ in
the world.
  Subpriority One: Evangelism.
  Subpriority Two: Social involvement.
    Sub-subpriority One: Social service.
    Sub-subpriority Two: Social action.

THE SEVEN VITAL SIGNS

Vital signs were identified by medical science to describe what happens inside a healthy human being. Vital signs are also useful to diagnose ill health. Churches also have vital signs—seven of them. A recognition of these signs and their implications leads to an understanding of what happens within healthy, growing churches.

If your church is growing, it will probably score high on most of the seven vital signs. If not, a good place to start the diagnosis would be to measure your church against these signs and try to find where the greatest deviation is taking place.

So here again is a list of the seven vital signs:

1. *A pastor who is a possibility thinker and whose dynamic leadership has been used to catalyze the entire church into action for growth.*
2. *A well-mobilized laity which has discovered, has developed, and is using all the spiritual gifts for growth.*
3. *A church big enough to provide the range of services that meet the needs and expectations of its members.*
4. *The proper balance of the dynamic relationship between celebration, congregation, and cell.*
5. *A membership drawn primarily from one homogeneous unit.*

6. *Evangelistic methods that have been proved to make disciples.*
7. *Priorities arranged in biblical order.*

STUDY QUESTIONS

1. What are the priorities of your church? Are they clearly stated? What are your personal priorities concerning evangelization of the world? What do you feel a church ought to be doing concerning social needs of the community? Do you agree with the author that salvation and the ultimate meaning of life is the highest priority of the church?

2. Do you agree with Jack Hyles's stated priorities that evangelism comes first and social needs must be met secondarily? How is your church relating to these priorities? Are you meeting the needs of people by evangelizing and meeting their social needs?

3. What do you feel about the author's conclusion of social service versus social action? Do you think he has established the correct priorities? If so, how should this impact your church and its priorities?

Chapter 12

GOD WANTS YOUR CHURCH TO GROW!

Every so often I get irked at some of my colleagues in the ministry. I don't mind debating the principles of church growth. Whenever I do I learn something more about why some churches grow and why some decline. I don't mind pastors of static or declining churches honestly seeking out reasons why it is happening; in fact I spend a good bit of my time encouraging such self-diagnosis.

But when ministers associated with declining churches come up with *biblical* rationalizations for their lack of growth, I confess I get irritated. It is simply biblical and theological nonsense to argue that God is pleased when churches, year after year and generation after generation lose members.

IS CHURCH GROWTH THE POINT?

I refer again to Robert Hudnut's book, *Church Growth Is Not the Point* (Harper and Row). Here is a whole book attempting to muster theological reasons why God prefers churches to lose members rather than to gain them. He notices that people are leaving the church and says that "it

could not be a better sign." In many cases, "loss of growth
in statistics has meant increase in growth in the gospel."
He rejoices that declining churches get rid of "dead wood"
and stay with the "faithful remnant." "Church growth is
not the point," he stresses, "faithfulness to our Lord Jesus
Christ is."

This is a theological slight of hand.   Notice that Hudnut tries to set church growth *against* the gospel. He even
tries to set it *against* faithfulness to Jesus Christ! Those
familiar with the New Testament need no detailed answer
to such an unbiblical line of reasoning. They know that
Jesus commanded church growth, and that Christians who
are faithful to Him as Lord will work toward that goal.

The gospel is to be proclaimed to all nations, and the
expected response is repentance and faith in Christ. Jesus
told us to baptize these people in the name of the Father
and the Son and the Holy Ghost (Matt. 28:19), and if that
doesn't mean church growth, I don't know what does.

A pastor in Southern California wrote an article
attempting to set church growth against *evangelism,* of all
things. He is disturbed because "evangelism has always
been connected with church growth." He considers evangelism to be a much bigger term than that. "It certainly
must mean more than the recruitment of persons into the
life of the church," he argues.

"We count heads," this pastor says. "God counts
hearts." He suggests that we have a one-year moratorium
on statistics so that we can get down to the business of
evangelism. He feels that God's strategy might not be to
extend the Kingdom of God, but rather to *intensify* it.

Two biblical illustrations are given to buttress this
rather unusual view of what evangelism might be. The
first is of Gideon who reduced an original thirty-two thousand volunteers to a corps of three hundred in order to
attack the Midianites. The second is of our Lord who,

though great crowds were drawn by His preaching, required that His disciples bear a cross, and ended up dying alone.

Gideon? Evangelism? Certainly Gideon was a hero. His tricky strategy which routed and defeated the Midianites was all part of God's plan for the Israel of that day. But to make this wartime episode a paradigm for understanding New Testament evangelism is highly questionable.

For each example of Gideon's battle tactics, the Bible has dozens of examples of Joshua's style which threw as many warriors as possible into the thick of the battle. Throughout history wars have generally been won by large armies. By the same token world evangelism has been best accomplished when, to use another analogy, the Lord of the harvest has thrust out laborers into the harvest field in great numbers. Or else why would Jesus say, "Therefore pray the Lord of the harvest to send out laborers into His harvest" (Matt. 9:38)?

JESUS AND CHURCH GROWTH

Relating Gideon to evangelism and church growth requires mental gymnastics of which I am not capable. But relating Jesus Himself to evangelism and church growth is something else. After all, Jesus came "to seek and to save that which was lost" (Luke 19:10).

Jesus believed in statistics enough to suggest that the good pastor is the one who knows his sheep so well that he noticed that out of a hundred sheep, one was missing. And when one was missing, Jesus' idea of a good shepherd was not to say, "Oh, that was just a weak sheep: the flock will be better off without him." No, that shepherd went out and searched for the lost sheep until he found it and brought it back (Luke 15:4-6).

The story of the lost sheep is related directly to evangelism. Jesus says that lost persons need to be sought and found and brought into the fold. When that happens, He says that there is great joy in heaven (Luke 15:7).

Jesus also said, "I will build My church, and the gates of Hades shall not prevail against it" (Matt. 16:18). He was all in favor of church growth. When He talked about the Kingdom of God, He talked about a tiny mustard seed which would eventually develop into a great tree (Matt. 13:31-32). Growth again!

Jesus knew there would be tares among the wheat as the Kingdom of God grew, but He told His followers not to worry very much about the tares; Hudnut would call them "dead wood." "Let both grow together," He said, "until the harvest" (Matt. 13:30).

I have a hunch that many of these people whom pastors relegate to "dead wood" are in reality good Christian people who are leaving certain churches in America because (1) they or their families are hurting and need pastoral care they do not find in those churches, or (2) they are live Christians who find little or no opportunity for exercising their spiritual gifts in dull, declining churches.

Some of these people, unfortunately, may drift away from the faith. A large number of them, however, look for another church more adequately geared to meet their spiritual needs.

Sometimes when this change happens and when a number of people leave Church *A* and join Church *B*, Church *B* is accused of "sheep-stealing." In many cases, however, I think it might better be considered "sheep finding." When pastors like those we have been discussing say "good riddance to the dead wood" as men and women leave their churches, those men and women become sheep without a shepherd. And blessings on the shepherd who is willing to seek them and find them and fold them into a loving congregation.

The next step is for Church *A* to call a moratorium on

statistics so that when the year ends the leaders of that church have no idea how many of their sheep might have been lost. This protects shepherds who care little whether the wolves come in and raid the flock since there is no way they can be held accountable without statistics. But I do not see Jesus commending such a procedure, and I do not feel that lack of church growth should be dignified by attributing it to the will of God.

WAS JESUS "SUCCESS-ORIENTED"?

But if Jesus' will was church growth, how did He do? What kind of success did He have? Was He "success-oriented" at all?

After all, Jesus did end up on a cross. And His disciples had either abandoned Him or were watching from afar off. What does all this say to the Church Growth Movement?

Notice that the cross was never an end in itself. It was the means toward another end. Jesus died as the Lamb of God who takes away the sins of the world. He was sacrificed to pay the price of human sins, and He was eminently successful in doing so.

Since He died, the blood of Jesus Christ has been sufficient to cleanse us from all sin (1 John 1:7). People who repent of their sins and believe in the power of Jesus' blood to forgive their sins are saved. They become "new creatures in Christ" (2 Cor. 5:17), and as such they are called "disciples." Disciples are added to the church of Jesus Christ.

In plain language, therefore, one way of looking at the purpose of Jesus' death on the cross is that it provides the means through which church growth can happen. When men and women are saved, churches grow.

So far, so good. But did Jesus *succeed* at this? Did He give us an example of evangelism and church growth to follow?

I have seen some people wring their hands and make excuses for Jesus at this point. "Well," they sometimes say, "Jesus might not have done much, but He promised us that we would do greater things." Some even compare Jesus unfavorably to the superchurch pastors in the world today.

In my opinion, Jesus needs no apology. As an evangelist He was an outstanding success. He was a missionary to unreached peoples. Yet only three years elapsed between the start and the finish of his active ministry.

Jesus began by winning twelve people to Himself. When He finished, the Twelve had become a committed group in Jerusalem of no less than 120 disciples, but more probably upwards of 600—as hinted in 1 Corinthians 15:6. Growth from twelve to 120 in three years represents a decadal rate of 215,343 percent or an annual growth rate of 115 percent! This is astronomical enough without even figuring it on the basis of 600 instead of 120!

Granted, these figures are not too useful in themselves, since everyone knows that when you start with a small number like twelve, the rates of growth become enormous. The proof of the pudding comes in whether high rates of growth can be *sustained* after such a propitious beginning.

GROWTH IN THE BOOK OF ACTS

What do you suppose happened to the church Jesus planted in Jerusalem? Did the leaders say, "Let's now see if we can do what Gideon did and reduce the 120 to 40 or 50 before we start evangelizing?" No, instead they waited and prayed only until the whole 120 were filled with the Holy Spirit and all of them began to proclaim the gospel with vigor. What happened after that is a matter of record in the book of Acts, which I take much more as an example of God's will for a healthy church than the story of Gideon or the dark moments on Calvary.

And what exactly does the book of Acts say happened to this little church that Jesus left behind?

"Then those who gladly received his word were baptized; and that day about three thousand souls were added to them" (2:41).

This was the day of Pentecost. Peter and the apostles did their jobs as evangelists. The rest of the 120 exercised their spiritual gifts and nurtured the new converts. When people repented and were baptized the church grew by leaps and bounds. Growth was so rapid that it would be next to ridiculous to figure annual or decadal rates on the basis of 120 to 3,120 in one day.

These three thousand were really disciples. The fact that there was considerable quantity did not seem to reduce the quality. They "continued steadfastly in the apostles' doctrine and fellowship, in the breaking of bread, and in prayers" (Acts 2:42).

"And the Lord added to the church daily those who were being saved" (2:47).

Pentecost was no flash in the pan. The Jerusalem church did not make the mistake of saying, "We've finished our evangelism. Let's now enter into a period of consolidation." Jesus had taught church growth principles well enough so that they knew they shouldn't separate evangelism and follow-up. While nurturing new believers and building their faith, they simultaneously kept evangelizing. As a result, new believers joined the church every day.

How many were added this way? Luke doesn't tell us, but would it be far off to postulate another three thousand? That would make six thousand total. The next passage does give an exact figure:

"However, many of those who heard the word believed; and the number of the men came to be about five thousand " (4:4).

So much was happening by now, that government officials became concerned. Peter and John were put into prison for their bold evangelistic preaching, but not before they had won five thousand men alone.

How many women might have been saved also? Perhaps another five thousand? And could we count one child for each man and woman? If so, we are probably looking at up to fifteen thousand disciples at this point.

"And the word of God spread, and the number of the disciples multiplied greatly in Jerusalem" (6:7).

In two of the three passages quoted above, the word "added" was used. But the church continued to grow so rapidly that *addition* of disciples now became *multiplication.* Possibly the 215,343 percent decadal rate we calculated previously wasn't too far off after all.

The Jerusalem church had grown so rapidly at this point that precise figures are impossible. But it seems quite clear that by the time Acts 6 and the persecution came along the church had grown from an original 120 to something up to 25,000.

The Great Commission was being fulfilled. The early disciples who knew Jesus personally, interpreted faithfulness to Jesus, at least in part, as actively spreading the Good News and planting new churches.

A good start had been made in Jerusalem. But the Commission said, "You shall be witnesses to Me in Jerusalem, and in all Judea and Samaria, and to the end of the earth" (Acts 1:8). So, from Jerusalem and Judea, they moved out into Samaria!

And then what happened?

"But when they believed Philip as he preached the things concerning the kingdom of God and the name of Jesus Christ, both men and women were baptized" (Acts 8:12).

Here we find Philip the evangelist—who in all probability had not even been a Christian when Jesus was crucified—chased out of Jerusalem by the persecution and now planting churches in Samaria. He went from village to village and the church grew magnificently among those people traditionally so despised by the Jews.

"Then the churches throughout all Judea, Galilee, and Samaria had peace and were edified. And walking in the fear of the Lord and in the comfort of the Holy Spirit, they were multiplied" (9:31).

By this time the gospel had reached Galilee and churches had been planted there. The interesting thing here is that previously Luke had spoken of *people* being first added, then multiplied, but now the movement is spreading so fast that he speaks of *churches* being multiplied.

"So all who dwelt at Lydda and Sharon saw him and turned to the Lord" (9:35).

Something new happened here. Through Peter, a paralyzed man was healed and, as a result, two entire villages decided as groups to follow Christ. The phenomenon of people movements to Christ has since become an important part of church growth philosophy, even though people movements are rather unusual in the U.S. and Canada today. In other parts of the world, however, multitudes are becoming Christians through people movements similar to those in Lydda and Sharon.

"And the hand of the Lord was with them, and a great number believed and turned to the Lord" (11:21).

This passage signals the beginning of church growth among the Gentiles. Previously churches were being multiplied among Jews and Samaritans, but here in Antioch the Gentiles began their time of coming to the Lord. The political situation of that day virtually ended the Christian movement among Jews before the first century was over, but what began in Antioch among Gentiles has continued at an accelerated rate ever since.

"Now a certain woman named Lydia heard us. She was a seller of purple from the city of Thyatira, who worshiped God. The Lord opened her heart" (16:14).

This passage concerning the church at Philippi is significant because it marks the beginning of church planting in Europe. This new growth resulted as the gospel spread among Gentiles from Antioch through the missionary activities of Paul, Barnabas and others. And since the ancestors of many Americans were Europeans, the church at Philippi will always hold a special place in their experience.

"And when they heard it, they glorified the Lord. And they said to him, 'You see, brother, how many myriads of Jews there are who have believed, and they are all zealous for the law'" (21:20).

The word translated "myriads" in this passage comes from the Greek word meaning "tens of thousands." In other words, toward the close of the ministry of the Apostle Paul—who spent most of his time evangelizing and planting new churches among the Gentiles—the number of Jews who had become followers of Jesus could only be estimated in myriads or multiples of ten thousand.

Could the total figure have been something around 100 thousand? Just for curiosity, if it were 100 thousand and the period of time since Pentecost were calculated at thirty years, that Jerusalem Church which started with 3,120 on Pentecost sustained a decadal growth rate of 222 percent, superb in anyone's book. This says nothing about the results of the ministry of Paul, Barnabas, and others who concentrated on the Gentiles.

JESUS WAS SUCCESSFUL

So, whether one likes to think of Jesus as "success-oriented" or not, His stated goal of making disciples was a tremendous success for at least thirty years after He

planted the first church and went to heaven. Any missionary or evangelist I know would like to be able to report
success in similar terms. Not only did Jesus die on the
cross for church growth and command church growth, but
He also set an example for church growth through His
ministry.

This should make the followers of Jesus today tremendously optimistic. God's will is clear. The same Holy Spirit
who filled the believers and set them preaching the gospel
on Pentecost is here and available today. The Christian
movement has spread worldwide so that today every
nation in the world now has a community of those who
claim Jesus Christ as their Lord and Saviour.

By a conservative estimate, seventy-eight thousand
people become Christians every day. Every week at least
sixteen hundred new Christian churches are planted
around the world.

The harvest is out there, in quantities far too great for
the available reapers. Here in the United States it is estimated that at least 100 million people have yet to commit
their lives to Jesus as Lord. Not all of them are receptive,
but tens of millions are. Chances are that within a short
driving distance of your own church are thousands and
thousands of people who need the Lord and who would
become faithful disciples if they heard the gospel in terms
they could understand and relate to.

YOU CAN BE SUCCESSFUL, TOO

Many people will not become Christians unless and
until your church and hundreds of other churches like
yours take seriously the command of Christ to make disciples of all nations. You and your church can participate in
the harvest. You can win people to Christ and bring them
into responsible church membership.

But it will not happen just because you wish it to.

Cases of easy, spontaneous evangelism can be found, but the world will not be won by Christians enjoying each other and waiting for it to happen. Discipleship is costly. Effective evangelism is costly. Part of taking up your cross is seeing to it that what you do contributes to others taking up their crosses also.

God's work in the world today will not be accomplished by timid, pessimistic people who rationalize away defeat. It will only be done by those who are sold out for God!

Friend, God wants you and the Christians around you turned on for Him. One of the things He wants to use you for is to reach out in love to unbelievers in your community and bring them to Jesus. He wants you filled with the Spirit. He wants others to know and love Him. He wants to add daily to your church such as should be saved.

God wants your church to grow, and because of that, your church can grow!

STUDY QUESTIONS

1. Review again the author's scriptural basis for concluding that the church must grow. Do you agree that it was Jesus' intent that the church would grow and that this process would be directly related to the evangelization of the unsaved? What was the significance of Jesus' death on the cross as it relates to church growth?

2. Did you trace the author's teaching through the book of Acts concerning church growth? What did you see in terms of the keeping of numbers? Does the Bible actually indicate a results-orientation in its philosophy of evangelizing? Is the Great Commission fulfilled then only by the winning of new people to Christ and bringing them into a countable relationship in the Church?

3. What did you think about the statement that "seventy-eight thousand people became Christians every day," and "every week at least sixteen hundred new Christian churches" are started? How does this news impact your thinking in relationship to church growth and to having new church offspring from your church?

INDEX